EFFECTIVE
SOFTWARE
TESTING

EFFECTIVE
SOFTWARE
TESTING

50 Specific Ways to Improve Your Testing

ELFRIEDE DUSTIN

✦ Addison-Wesley

Boston • San Francisco • New York • Toronto • Montreal
London • Munich • Paris • Madrid
Capetown • Sydney • Tokyo • Singapore • Mexico City

The publisher offers discounts on this book when ordered in quantity for bulk purchases and special sales. For more information, please contact:

U.S. Corporate and Government Sales
(800) 382-3419
corpsales@pearsontechgroup.com

For sales outside of the U.S., please contact:

International Sales
(317) 581-3793
international@pearsontechgroup.com

Visit Addison-Wesley on the Web: www.awprofessional.com

Library of Congress Cataloging-in-Publication Data
Dustin, Elfriede.
  Effective software testing : 50 specific ways to improve your testing / Elfriede Dustin.
    p. cm.
  Includes bibliographical references and index.
  ISBN 0-201-79429-2
  1. Computer software--Testing. I. Title.

  QA76.76.T48 D873 2002
  005.1'4—dc21

                                                                2002014338

ISBN 0201794292
Text printed in the United States at Offset Paperback Manufacturers in Laflin, Pennsylvania.
Printing 4 May, 2006.

To Jackie, Erika, and Cedric

Contents

Preface   xi

Acknowledgments   xv

1. Requirements Phase   1

Item 1: Involve Testers from the Beginning   3

Item 2: Verify the Requirements   5

Item 3: Design Test Procedures As Soon As Requirements Are Available   11

Item 4: Ensure That Requirement Changes Are Communicated   15

Item 5: Beware of Developing and Testing Based on an Existing System   19

2. Test Planning   23

Item 6: Understand the Task At Hand and the Related Testing Goal   25

Item 7: Consider the Risks   31

Item 8: Base Testing Efforts on a Prioritized Feature Schedule   39

Item 9: Keep Software Issues in Mind   41

Item 10: Acquire Effective Test Data   43

Item 11: Plan the Test Environment   47

Item 12: Estimate Test Preparation and Execution Time   51

3. The Testing Team   63

Item 13: Define Roles and Responsibilities   65

Item 14: Require a Mixture of Testing Skills,
Subject-Matter Expertise, and Experience   75

Item 15: Evaluate the Tester's Effectiveness   79

4. The System Architecture   91

Item 16: Understand the Architecture and
Underlying Components   93

Item 17: Verify That the System Supports Testability   97

Item 18: Use Logging to Increase System Testability   99

Item 19: Verify That the System Supports Debug
and Release Execution Modes   103

5. Test Design and Documentation   107

Item 20: Divide and Conquer   109

Item 21: Mandate the Use of a Test-Procedure
Template and Other Test-Design Standards   115

Item 22: Derive Effective Test Cases from Requirements   121

Item 23: Treat Test Procedures As "Living" Documents   125

Item 24: Utilize System Design and Prototypes   127

Item 25: Use Proven Testing Techniques when
Designing Test-Case Scenarios   129

Item 26: Avoid Including Constraints and Detailed
Data Elements within Test Procedures   135

Item 27: Apply Exploratory Testing   139

6. Unit Testing   143

Item 28: Structure the Development Approach to
Support Effective Unit Testing   145

Item 29: Develop Unit Tests in Parallel or Before
the Implementation   151

Item 30: Make Unit-Test Execution Part of the
Build Process   155

7. Automated Testing Tools   159

Item 31: Know the Different Types of
Testing-Support Tools   161

Item 32: Consider Building a Tool Instead of Buying One 167

Item 33: Know the Impact of Automated Tools
        on the Testing Effort   171
Item 34: Focus on the Needs of Your Organization   177
Item 35: Test the Tools on an Application Prototype   183

8. Automated Testing: Selected Best Practices   185

Item 36: Do Not Rely Solely on Capture/Playback   187
Item 37: Develop a Test Harness When Necessary   191
Item 38: Use Proven Test-Script Development Techniques   197
Item 39: Automate Regression Tests When Feasible   201
Item 40: Implement Automated Builds and Smoke Tests   207

9. Nonfunctional Testing   211

Item 41: Do Not Make Nonfunctional Testing
        an Afterthought   213
Item 42: Conduct Performance Testing with
        Production-Sized Databases   217
Item 43: Tailor Usability Tests to the Intended Audience   221
Item 44: Consider All Aspects of Security, for
        Specific Requirements and System-Wide   225
Item 45: Investigate the System's Implementation
        To Plan for Concurrency Tests   229
Item 46: Set Up an Efficient Environment for
        Compatibility Testing   235

10. Managing Test Execution   239

Item 47: Clearly Define the Beginning and End of the
        Test-Execution Cycle   241
Item 48: Isolate the Test Environment from the
        Development Environment   245
Item 49: Implement a Defect-Tracking Life Cycle   247
Item 50: Track the Execution of the Testing Program   255

Index   259

Preface

I n most software-development organizations, the testing program functions as the final "quality gate" for an application, allowing or preventing the move from the comfort of the software-engineering environment into the real world. With this role comes a large responsibility: The success of an application, and possibly of the organization, can rest on the quality of the software product.

A multitude of small tasks must be performed and managed by the testing team—so many, in fact, that it is tempting to focus purely on the mechanics of testing a software application and pay little attention to the surrounding tasks required of a testing program. Issues such as the acquisition of proper test data, testability of the application's requirements and architecture, appropriate test-procedure standards and documentation, and hardware and facilities are often addressed very late, if at all, in a project's life cycle. For projects of any significant size, test scripts and tools alone will not suffice—a fact to which most experienced software testers will attest.

Knowledge of what constitutes a successful end-to-end testing effort is typically gained through experience. The realization that a testing program could have been much more effective had certain tasks been performed earlier in the project life cycle is a valuable lesson. Of course, at that point, it's usually too late for the current project to benefit from the experience.

Effective Software Testing provides experience-based practices and key concepts that can be used by an organization to implement a successful and efficient testing program. The goal is to provide a distilled collection of techniques and discussions that can be directly applied by software personnel to improve their products and avoid costly mistakes and oversights. This book details 50 specific software testing best practices, contained in ten parts that roughly follow the software life cycle. This structure itself illustrates a key concept in software testing: To be most effective, the testing effort must be integrated into the software-development process as a whole. Isolating the testing effort into one box in the "work flow" (at the end of the software life cycle) is a common mistake that must be avoided.

The material in the book ranges from process- and management-related topics, such as managing changing requirements and the makeup of the testing team, to technical aspects such as ways to improve the testability of the system and the integration of unit testing into the development process. Although some pseudocode is given where necessary, the content is not tied to any particular technology or application platform.

It is important to note that there are factors outside the scope of the testing program that bear heavily on the success or failure of a project. Although a complete software-development process with its attendant testing program will ensure a successful engineering effort, any project must also deal with issues relating to the business case, budgets, schedules, and the culture of the organization. In some cases, these issues will be at odds with the needs of an effective engineering environment. The recommendations in this book assume that the organization is capable of adapting, and providing the support to the testing program necessary for its success.

ORGANIZATION

This book is organized into 50 separate items covering ten important areas. The selected best practices are organized in a sequence that parallels the phases of the system development life cycle.

The reader can approach the material sequentially, item-by-item and part-by-part, or simply refer to specific items when necessary to gain information about and understanding of a particular problem. For the most part, each chapter stands on its own, although there are references to other chapters, and other books, where helpful to provide the reader with additional information.

Chapter 1 describes requirements-phase considerations for the testing effort. It is important in the requirements phase for all stakeholders, including a representative of the testing team, to be involved in and informed of all requirements and changes. In addition, basing test cases on requirements is an essential concept for any large project. The importance of having the testing team represented during this phase cannot be overstated; it is in this phase that a thorough understanding of the system and its requirements can be obtained.

Chapter 2 covers test-planning activities, including ways to gain understanding of the goals of the testing effort, approaches to determining the test strategy, and considerations related to data, environments, and the software itself. Planning must take place as early as possible in the software life cycle, as lead times must be considered for implementing the test program successfully. Early planning allows for testing schedules and budgets to be estimated, approved, and incorporated into the overall software development plan. Estimates must be continually monitored and compared to actuals, so they can be revised and expectations can be managed as required.

Chapter 3 focuses on the makeup of the testing team. At the core of any successful testing program are its people. A successful testing team has a mixture of technical and domain knowledge, as well as a structured and concise division of roles and responsibilities. Continually evaluating the effectiveness of each test-team member throughout the testing process is important to ensuring success.

Chapter 4 discusses architectural considerations for the system under test. Often overlooked, these factors must be taken into account to ensure that the system itself is testable, and to enable gray-box testing and effective defect diagnosis.

Chapter 5 details the effective design and development of test procedures, including considerations for the creation and documentation of tests, and discusses the most effective testing techniques. As requirements and system design are refined over time and through system-development iterations, so must the test procedures be refined to incorporate the new or modified requirements and system functions.

Chapter 6 examines the role of developer unit testing in the overall testing strategy. Unit testing in the implementation phase can result in significant gains in software quality. If unit testing is done properly, later testing phases will be more successful. There is a difference, however, between casual, ad-hoc unit testing based on knowledge of the problem, and structured, repeatable unit testing based on the requirements of the system.

Chapter 7 explains automated testing tool issues, including the proper types of tools to use on a project, the build-versus-buy decision, and factors to consider in selecting the right tool for the organization. The numerous types of testing tools available for use throughout the phases in the development life cycle are described here. In addition, custom tool development is also covered.

Chapter 8 discusses selected best practices for automated testing. The proper use of capture/playback tools, test harnesses, and regression testing are described.

Chapter 9 provides information on testing nonfunctional aspects of a software application. Ensuring that nonfunctional requirements are met, including performance, security, usability, compatibility, and concurrency testing, adds to the overall quality of the application.

Chapter 10 provides a strategy for managing the execution of tests, including appropriate methods of tracking test-procedure execution and the defect life cycle, and gathering metrics to assess the testing process.

AUDIENCE

The target audience of this book includes Quality Assurance professionals, software testers, and test leads and managers. Much of the information presented can also be of value to project managers and software developers looking to improve the quality of a software project.

Acknowledgments

My thanks to all of the software professionals who helped support the development of this book, including students attending my tutorials on Automated Software Testing, Quality Web Systems, and Effective Test Management; my co-workers on various testing efforts at various companies; and the co-authors of my various writings. Their valuable questions, insights, feedback, and suggestions have directly and indirectly added value to the content of this book. I especially thank Douglas McDiarmid for his valuable contributions to this effort. His input has greatly added to the content, presentation, and overall quality of the material.

My thanks also to the following individuals, whose feedback was invaluable: Joe Strazzere, Gerald Harrington, Karl Wiegers, Ross Collard, Bob Binder, Wayne Pagot, Bruce Katz, Larry Fellows, Steve Paulovich, and Tim Van Tongeren.

I want to thank the executives at Addison-Wesley for their support of this project, especially Debbie Lafferty, Mike Hendrickson, John Fuller, Chris Guzikowski, and Elizabeth Ryan.

Last but not least, my thanks to Eric Brown, who designed the interesting book cover.

Elfriede Dustin

CHAPTER 1
Requirements Phase

The most effective testing programs start at the beginning of a project, long before any program code has been written. The requirements documentation is verified first; then, in the later stages of the project, testing can concentrate on ensuring the quality of the application code. Expensive reworking is minimized by eliminating requirements-related defects early in the project's life, prior to detailed design or coding work.

The requirements specifications for a software application or system must ultimately describe its functionality in great detail. One of the most challenging aspects of requirements development is communicating with the people who are supplying the requirements. Each requirement should be stated precisely and clearly, so it can be understood in the same way by everyone who reads it.

If there is a consistent way of documenting requirements, it is possible for the stakeholders responsible for requirements gathering to effectively participate in the requirements process. As soon as a requirement is made visible, it can be **tested** and clarified by asking the stakeholders detailed questions. A variety of **requirement tests** can be applied to ensure that each requirement is relevant, and that everyone has the same understanding of its meaning.

Item 1: Involve Testers from the Beginning

Testers need to be involved from the beginning of a project's life cycle so they can understand exactly what they are testing and can work with other stakeholders to create testable requirements.

Defect prevention is the use of techniques and processes that can help detect and avoid errors before they propagate to later development phases. Defect prevention is most effective during the requirements phase, when the impact of a change required to fix a defect is low: The only modifications will be to requirements documentation and possibly to the testing plan, also being developed during this phase. If testers (along with other stakeholders) are involved from the beginning of the development life cycle, they can help recognize omissions, discrepancies, ambiguities, and other problems that may affect the project requirements' testability, correctness, and other qualities.

A requirement can be considered **testable** if it is possible to design a procedure in which the functionality being tested can be executed, the expected output is known, and the output can be programmatically or visually verified.

Testers need a solid understanding of the product so they can devise better and more complete test plans, designs, procedures, and cases. Early test-team involvement can eliminate confusion about functional behavior later in the project life cycle. In addition, early involvement allows the test team to learn over time which aspects of the application are the most critical to the end user and which are the highest-risk elements. This knowledge enables testers to focus on the most important parts of the application first, avoiding over-testing rarely used areas and under-testing the more important ones.

Some organizations regard testers strictly as consumers of the requirements and other software development work products, requiring them to learn the application and domain as software builds are delivered to the testers, instead of involving them during the earlier phases. This may be acceptable in smaller projects, but in complex environments it is not realistic to expect testers to find all significant defects if their first exposure to the application is after it has already been through requirements, analysis, design, and some software implementation. More than just understanding the "inputs and outputs" of the software, testers need deeper knowledge that can come only from understanding the *thought process* used during the specification of product functionality. Such understanding not only increases the quality and depth of the test procedures developed, but also allows testers to provide feedback regarding the requirements.

The earlier in the life cycle a defect is discovered, the cheaper it will be to fix it. Table 1.1 outlines the relative cost to correct a defect depending on the life-cycle stage in which it is discovered.[1]

Table 1.1. Prevention is Cheaper Than Cure: Error Removal Cost Multiplies over System Development Life Cycle

Phase	Relative Cost to Correct
Definition	$1
High-Level Design	$2
Low-Level Design	$5
Code	$10
Unit Test	$15
Integration Test	$22
System Test	$50
Post-Delivery	$100+

---

1. B. Littlewood, ed., *Software Reliability: Achievement and Assessment* (Henley-on-Thames, England: Alfred Waller, Ltd., November 1987).

Item 2: Verify the Requirements

In his work on specifying the requirements for buildings, Christopher Alexander[1] describes setting up a **quality measure** for each requirement: "The idea is for each requirement to have a quality measure that makes it possible to divide all solutions to the requirement into two classes: those for which we agree that they fit the requirement and those for which we agree that they do not fit the requirement." In other words, if a quality measure is specified for a requirement, any solution that meets this measure will be acceptable, and any solution that does not meet the measure will not be acceptable. Quality measures are used to test the new system against the requirements.

Attempting to define the quality measure for a requirement helps to rationalize fuzzy requirements. For example, everyone would agree with a statement like "the system must provide good value," but each person may have a different interpretation of "good value." In devising the scale that must be used to measure "good value," it will become necessary to identify what that term means. Sometimes requiring the stakeholders to think about a requirement in this way will lead to defining an agreed-upon quality measure. In other cases, there may be no agreement on a quality measure. One solution would be to replace one vague requirement with several unambiguous requirements, each with its own quality measure.[2]

It is important that guidelines for requirement development and documentation be defined at the outset of the project. In all but the smallest programs, careful

---

1. Christopher Alexander, *Notes On the Synthesis of Form* (Cambridge, Mass.: Harvard University Press, 1964).
2. Tom Gilb has developed a notation, called Planguage (for Planning Language), to specify such quality requirements. His forthcoming book *Competitive Engineering* describes Planguage.

analysis is required to ensure that the system is developed properly. **Use cases** are one way to document functional requirements, and can lead to more thorough system designs and test procedures. (In most of this book, the broad term **requirement** will be used to denote any type of specification, whether a use case or another type of description of functional aspects of the system.)

In addition to functional requirements, it is also important to consider nonfunctional requirements, such as performance and security, early in the process: They can determine the technology choices and areas of risk. Nonfunctional requirements do not endow the system with any specific functions, but rather constrain or further define how the system will perform any given function. Functional requirements should be specified along with their associated nonfunctional requirements. (Chapter 9 discusses nonfunctional requirements.)

Following is a checklist that can be used by testers during the requirements phase to verify the quality of the requirements.[3,4] Using this checklist is a first step toward trapping requirements-related defects as early as possible, so they don't propagate to subsequent phases, where they would be more difficult and expensive to find and correct. All stakeholders responsible for requirements should verify that requirements possess the following attributes.

- **Correctness** of a requirement is judged based on what the user wants. For example, are the rules and regulations stated correctly? Does the requirement exactly reflect the user's request? It is imperative that the end user, or a suitable representative, be involved during the requirements phase. Correctness can also be judged based on standards. Are the standards being followed?

- **Completeness** ensures that no necessary elements are missing from the requirement. The goal is to avoid omitting requirements simply because no one has asked the right questions or examined all of the pertinent source documents.

    Testers should insist that associated nonfunctional requirements, such as performance, security, usability, compatibility, and accessibility,[5] are described

---

3. Suzanne Robertson, "An Early Start To Testing: How To Test Requirements," paper presented at EuroSTAR 96, Amsterdam, December 2–6, 1996. Copyright 1996 The Atlantic Systems Guild Ltd. Used by permission of the author.
4. Karl Wiegers, *Software Requirements* (Redmond, Wash.: Microsoft Press, Sept. 1999).
5. Elfriede Dustin et al., "Nonfunctional Requirements," in *Quality Web Systems: Performance, Security, and Usability* (Boston, Mass.: Addison-Wesley, 2002), Sec. 2.5.

along with each functional requirement. Nonfunctional requirements are usually documented in two steps:

1. A system-wide specification is created that defines the nonfunctional requirements that apply to the system. For example, "The user interface of the Web system must be compatible with Netscape Navigator 4.x or higher and Microsoft Internet Explorer 4.x or higher."

2. Each requirement description should contain a section titled "Nonfunctional Requirements" documenting any specific nonfunctional needs of that particular requirement that deviate from the system-wide nonfunctional specification.

- **Consistency** verifies that there are no internal or external contradictions among the elements within the work products, or between work products. By asking the question, *"Does the specification define every essential subject-matter term used within the specification?"* we can determine whether the elements used in the requirement are clear and precise. For example, a requirements specification that uses the term "viewer" in many places, with different meanings depending on context, will cause problems during design or implementation. Without clear and consistent definitions, determining whether a requirement is correct becomes a matter of opinion.

- **Testability** (or **verifiability**) of the requirement confirms that it is possible to create a test for the requirement, and that an expected result is known and can be programmatically or visually verified. If a requirement cannot be tested or otherwise verified, this fact and its associated risks must be stated, and the requirement must be adjusted if possible so that it can be tested.

- **Feasibility** of a requirement ensures that it can can be implemented given the budget, schedules, technology, and other resources available.

- **Necessity** verifies that every requirement in the specification is relevant to the system. To test for relevance or necessity, the tester checks the requirement against the stated goals for the system. Does this requirement contribute to those goals? Would excluding this requirement prevent the system from meeting those goals? Are any other requirements dependent on this requirement? Some irrelevant requirements are not really requirements, but proposed solutions.

- **Prioritization** allows everyone to understand the relative value to stakeholders of the requirement. Pardee[6] suggests that a scale from 1 to 5 be used to specify the level of reward for good performance and penalty for bad performance on a requirement. If a requirement is absolutely vital to the success of the system, then it has a penalty of 5 and a reward of 5. A requirement that would be nice to have but is not really vital might have a penalty of 1 and a reward of 3. The overall value or importance stakeholders place on a requirement is the sum of its penalties and rewards—in the first case, 10, and in the second, 4. This knowledge can be used to make prioritization and trade-off decisions when the time comes to design the system. This approach needs to balance the perspective of the user (one kind of stakeholder) against the cost and technical risk associated with a proposed requirement (the perspective of the developer, another kind of stakeholder).[7]

- **Unambiguousness** ensures that requirements are stated in a precise and measurable way. The following is an example of an ambiguous requirement: "The system must respond quickly to customer inquiries." "Quickly" is innately ambiguous and subjective, and therefore renders the requirement untestable. A customer might think "quickly" means within 5 seconds, while a developer may think it means within 3 minutes. Conversely, a developer might think it means within 2 seconds and over-engineer a system to meet unnecessary performance goals.

- **Traceablity** ensures that each requirement is identified in such a way that it can be associated with all parts of the system where it is used. For any change to requirements, is it possible to identify all parts of the system where this change has an effect?

  To this point, each requirement has been considered as a separately identifiable, measurable entity. It is also necessary to consider the connections among requirements—to understand the effect of one requirement on others. There must be a way of dealing with a large number of requirements and the complex connections among them. Suzanne Robertson[8] suggests that rather than trying to tackle everything simultaneously, it is better to divide requirements into

---

6. William J. Pardee, *To Satisfy and Delight Your Customer: How to Manage for Customer Value* (New York, N.Y.: Dorset House, 1996).
7. For more information, see Karl Wiegers, *Software Requirements*, Ch. 13.
8. Suzanne Robertson, "An Early Start to Testing," op. cit.

manageable groups. This could be a matter of allocating requirements to subsystems, or to sequential releases based on priority. Once that is done, the connections can be considered in two phases: first the internal connections among the requirements in each group, then the connections among the groups. If the requirements are grouped in a way that minimizes the connections between groups, the complexity of tracing connections among requirements will be minimized.

Traceability also allows collection of information about individual requirements and other parts of the system that could be affected if a requirement changes, such as designs, code, tests, help screens, and so on. When informed of requirement changes, testers can make sure that all affected areas are adjusted accordingly.

As soon as a single requirement is available for review, it is possible to start testing that requirement for the aforementioned characteristics. Trapping requirements-related defects as early as they can be identified will prevent incorrect requirements from being incorporated in the design and implementation, where they will be more difficult and expensive to find and correct.[9]

After following these steps, the feature set of the application under development is now outlined and quantified, which allows for better organization, planning, tracking, and testing of each feature.

---

9. T. Capers Jones, *Assessment and Control of Software Risks* (Upper Saddle River, N.J.: Prentice Hall PTR, 1994).

Item 3: Design Test Procedures As Soon As Requirements Are Available

Just as software engineers produce design documents based on requirements, it is necessary for the testing team to design test procedures based on these requirements as well. In some organizations, the development of test procedures is pushed off until after a build of the software is delivered to the testing team, due either to lack of time or lack of properly specified requirements suitable for test-procedure design. This approach has inherent problems, including the possibility of requirement omissions or errors being discovered late in the cycle; software implementation issues, such as failure to satisfy a requirement; nontestability; and the development of incomplete test procedures.

Moving the test procedure development effort closer to the requirements phase of the process, rather than waiting until the software-development phase, allows for test procedures to provide benefits to the requirement-specification activity. During the course of developing a test procedure, certain oversights, omissions, incorrect flows, and other errors may be discovered in the requirements document, as testers attempt to walk through an interaction with the system at a very specific level, using sets of test data as input. This process obliges the requirement to account for variations in scenarios, as well as to specify a clear path through the interaction in all cases.

If a problem is uncovered in the requirement, that requirement will need to be reworked to account for this discovery. The earlier in the process such corrections are incorporated, the less likely it is that the corrections will affect software design or implementation.

As mentioned in Item 1, early detection equates to lower cost. If a requirement defect is discovered in later phases of the process, all stakeholders must change the requirement, design, and code, which will affect budgets, schedules, and possibly morale. However, if the defect is discovered during the requirements phase, repairing it is simply a matter of changing and reviewing the requirement text.

The process of identifying errors or omissions in a requirement through test-procedure definition is referred to as **verifying the requirement's testability**. If not enough information exists, or the information provided in the specification is too ambiguous to create a complete test procedure with its related test cases for relevant paths, the specification is not considered to be testable, and may not be suitable for software development. Whether a test can be developed for a requirement is a valuable check and should be considered part of the process of approving a requirement as complete. There are exceptions, where a requirement cannot immediately be verified programmatically or manually by executing a test. Such exceptions need to be explicitly stated. For example, fulfillment of a requirement that "all data files need to be stored for record-keeping for three years" cannot be immediately verified. However, it does need to be approved, adhered to, and tracked.

If a requirement cannot be verified, there is no guarantee that it will be implemented correctly. Being able to develop a test procedure that includes data inputs, steps to verify the requirement, and known expected outputs for each related requirement can assure requirement completeness by confirming that important requirement information is not missing, making the requirement difficult or even impossible to implement correctly and untestable. Developing test procedures for requirements early on allows for early discovery of nonverifiability issues.

Developing test procedures after a software build has been delivered to the testing team also risks incomplete test-procedure development because of intensive time pressure to complete the product's testing cycle. This can manifest in various ways: For example, the test procedure might be missing entirely; or it may not be thoroughly defined, omitting certain paths or data elements that may make a difference in the test outcome. As a result, defects might be missed. Or, the requirement may be incomplete, as described earlier, and not support the definition of the necessary test procedures, or even proper software development. Incomplete requirements often result in incomplete implementation.

Early evaluation of the testability of an application's requirements can be the basis for defining a testing strategy. While reviewing the testability of the requirements, testers might determine, for example, that using a capture/playback tool would be ideal, allowing execution of some of the tests in an automated fashion. Determining this early allows enough lead time to evaluate and implement automated testing tools.

To offer another example: During an early evaluation phase, it could be determined that some requirements relating to complex and diversified calculations may be more suitable tested with a custom test harness (see Item 37) or specialized scripts. Test harness development and other such test-preparation activities will require additional lead time before testing can begin.

Moving test procedures closer to the requirements-definition phase of an **iteration**[1] carries some additional responsibilities, however, including prioritizing test procedures based on requirements, assigning adequate personnel, and understanding the testing strategy. It is often a luxury, if not impossible, to develop all test procedures immediately for each requirement, because of time, budget, and personnel constraints. Ideally, the requirements and subject-matter expert testing teams are both responsible for creating example test scenarios as part of the requirements definition, including scenario outcomes (the expected results).

Test-procedure development must be prioritized based on an iterative implementation plan. If time constraints exist, test developers should start by developing test procedures for the requirements to be implemented first. They can then develop "draft" test procedures for all requirements to be completed later.

Requirements are often refined through review and analysis in an iterative fashion. It is very common that new requirement details and scenario clarifications surface during the design and development phase. Purists will say that all requirement details should be ironed out during the requirements phase. However, the reality is that deadline pressures require development to start as soon as possible; the luxury of having complete requirements up-front is rare. If requirements are refined later in the process, the associated test procedures also need to be refined. These also must be kept up-to-date with respect to any changes: They should be treated as "living" documents.

---

1. An **iteration**, used in an **iterative development process**, includes the activities of requirement analysis, design, implementation and testing. There are many iterations in an iterative development process. A single iteration for the whole project would be known as the **waterfall model**.

Effectively managing such evolving requirements and test procedures requires a well-defined process in which test designers are also stakeholders in the requirement process. See Item 4 for more on the importance of communicating requirement changes to all stakeholders.

Item 4: Ensure That Requirement Changes Are Communicated

When test procedures are based on requirements, it is important to keep test team members informed of changes to the requirements as they occur. This may seem obvious, but it is surprising how often test procedures are executed that differ from an application's implementation that has been changed due to updated requirements. Many times, testers responsible for developing and executing the test procedures are not notified of requirements changes, which can result in false reports of defects, and loss of required research and valuable time.

There can be several reasons for this kind of process breakdown, such as:

- *Undocumented changes.* Someone, for example the product or project manager, the customer, or a requirements analyst, has instructed the developer to implement a feature change, without agreement from other stakeholders, and the developer has implemented the change without communicating or documenting it. A process needs to be in place that makes it clear to the developer how and when requirements can be changed. This is commonly handled through a **Change Control Board**, an **Engineering Review Board**, or some similar mechanism, discussed below.

- *Outdated requirement documentation.* An oversight on the testers' part or poor configuration management may cause a tester to work with an outdated version of the requirement documentation when developing the test plan or procedures. Updates to requirements need to be documented, placed under configuration management control (**baselined**), and communicated to all stakeholders involved.

- *Software defects.* The developer may have implemented a requirement incorrectly, although the requirement documentation and the test documentation are correct.

In the last case, a defect report should be written. However, if a requirement change process is not being followed, it can be difficult to tell which of the aforementioned scenarios is actually occurring. Is the problem in the software, the requirement, the test procedure, or all of the above? To avoid guesswork, all requirement changes must be openly evaluated, agreed upon, and communicated to all stakeholders. This can be accomplished by having a **requirement-change process** in place that facilitates the communication of any requirement changes to all stakeholders.

If a requirement needs to be corrected, the change process must take into account the ripple effect upon design, code, and all associated documentation, including test documentation. To effectively manage this process, any changes should be baselined and versioned in a configuration-management system.

The change process outlines when, how, by whom, and where change requests are initiated. The process might specify that a change request can be initiated during any phase of the life cycle—during any type of review, walk-through, or inspection during the requirements, design, code, defect tracking, or testing activities, or any other phase.

Each change request could be documented via a **change-request form**—a template listing all information necessary to facilitate the change-request process—which is passed on to the **Change Control Board** (CCB). Instituting a CCB helps ensure that any changes to requirements and other change requests follow a specific process. A CCB verifies that change requests are documented appropriately, evaluated, and agreed upon; that any affected documents (requirements, design documents, etc.) are updated; and that all stakeholders are informed of the change.

The CCB usually consists of representatives from the various management teams, e.g., product management, requirements management, and QA teams, as well as the testing manager and the configuration manager. CCB meetings can be conducted on an as-needed basis. All stakeholders need to evaluate change proposals by analyzing the priority, risks, and tradeoffs associated with the suggested change.

Associated and critical impact analysis of the proposed change must also be performed. For example, a requirements change may affect the entire suite of testing documentation, requiring major additions to the test environment and extending the testing by numerous weeks. Or an implementation may need to be changed in a way that affects the entire automated testing suite. Such impacts must be identified, communicated, and addressed before the change is approved.

The CCB determines whether a change request's validity, effects, necessity, and priority (for example, whether it should be implemented immediately, or whether it can be documented in the project's central repository as an enhancement). The CCB must ensure that the suggested changes, associated risk evaluation, and decision-making processes are documented and communicated.

It is imperative that all parties be made aware of any change suggestions, allowing them to contribute to risk analysis and mitigation of change. An effective way to ensure this is to use a **requirements-management tool,**[1] which can be used to track the requirements changes as well as maintain the traceability of the requirements to the test procedures (see the testability checklist in Item 2 for a discussion of traceability). If the requirement changes, the change should be reflected and updated in the requirements-management tool, and the tool should mark the affected test artifact (and other affected elements, such as design, code, etc.), so the respective parties can update their products accordingly. All stakeholders can then get the latest information via the tool.

Change information managed with a requirements-management tool allows testers to reevaluate the testability of the changed requirement as well as the impact of changes to test artifacts (test plan, design, etc.) or the testing schedule. The affected test procedures must be revisited and updated to reflect the requirements and implementation changes. Previously identified defects must be reevaluated to determine whether the requirement change has made them obsolete. If scripts, test harnesses, or other testing mechanisms have already been created, they may need to be updated as well.

A well-defined process that facilitates communication of changed requirements, allowing for an effective test program, is critical to the efficiency of the project.

---

1. There are numerous excellent requirement management tools on the market, such as Rational's RequisitePro, QSS's DOORS, and Integrated Chipware's RTM: Requirement & Traceability Management.

Item 5: Beware of Developing and Testing Based on an Existing System

In many software-development projects, a legacy application already exists, with little or no existing requirement documentation, and is the basis for an architectural redesign or platform upgrade. Most organizations in this situation insist that the new system be developed and tested based exclusively on continual investigation of the existing application, without taking the time to analyze or document how the application functions. On the surface, it appears this will result in an earlier delivery date, since little or no effort is "wasted" on requirements reengineering or on analyzing and documenting an application that already exists, when the existing application in itself supposedly manifests the needed requirements.

Unfortunately, in all but the smallest projects, the strategy of using an existing application as the requirements baseline comes with many pitfalls and often results in few (if any) documented requirements, improper functionality, and incomplete testing.

Although some functional aspects of an application are self-explanatory, many domain-related features are difficult to reverse-engineer, because it is easy to overlook business logic that may depend on the supplied data. As it is usually not feasible to investigate the existing application with every possible data input, it is likely that some intricacy of the functionality will be missed. In some cases, the reasons for certain inputs producing certain outputs may be puzzling, and will result in software developers providing a "best guess" as to why the application behaves the way it does. To make matters worse, once the actual business logic is determined, it is typically not documented; instead, it is coded directly into the new application, causing the guessing cycle to perpetuate.

Aside from business-logic issues, it is also possible to misinterpret the meaning of user-interface fields, or miss whole sections of user interface completely.

Many times, the existing baseline application is still live and under development, probably using a different architecture along with an older technology (for example, desktop vs. Web versions); or it is in production and under continuous maintenance, which often includes defect fixing and feature additions for each new production release. This presents a "moving-target" problem: Updates and new features are being applied to the application that is to serve as the requirements baseline for the new product, even as it is being reverse-engineered by the developers and testers for the new application. The resulting new application may become a mixture of the different states of the existing application as it has moved through its own development life cycle.

Finally, performing analysis, design, development, and test activities in a "moving-target" environment makes it difficult to properly estimate time, budgets, and staffing required for the entire software development life cycle. The team responsible for the new application cannot effectively predict the effort involved, as no requirements are available to clarify what to build or test. Most estimates must be based on a casual understanding of the application's functionality that may be grossly incorrect, or may need to suddenly change if the existing application is upgraded. Estimating tasks is difficult enough when based on an excellent statement of requirements, but it is almost impossible when so-called "requirements" are embodied in a legacy or moving-target application.

On the surface, it may appear that one of the benefits of building an application based on an existing one is that testers can compare the "old" application's output over time to that produced by the newly implemented application, if the outputs are supposed to be the same. However, this can be unsafe: What if the "old" application's output has been wrong for some scenarios for a while, but no one has noticed? If the new application is behaving correctly, but the old application's output is wrong, the tester would document an invalid defect, and the resulting fix would incorporate the error present in the existing application.

If testers decide they can't rely on the "old" application for output comparison, problems remain. Or if they execute their test procedures and the output differs between the two applications, the testers are left wondering which output is correct. If the requirements are not documented, how can a tester know for certain which output is correct? The analysis that should have taken place during the requirements phase to determine the expected output is now in the hands of the tester.

Although basing a new software development project on an existing application can be difficult, there are ways to handle the situation. The first step is to manage expectations. Team members should be aware of the issues involved in basing new development on an existing application. The following list outlines several points to consider.

- *Use a fixed application version.* All stakeholders must understand why the new application must be based on one specific version of the existing software as described and must agree to this condition. The team must select a version of the existing application on which the new development is to be based, and use only that version for the initial development.

  Working from a fixed application version makes tracking defects more straightforward, since the selected version of the existing application will determine whether there is a defect in the new application, regardless of upgrades or corrections to the existing application's code base. It will still be necessary to verify that the existing application is indeed correct, using domain expertise, as it is important to recognize if the new application is correct while the legacy application is defective.

- *Document the existing application.* The next step is to have a domain or application expert document the existing application, writing at least a paragraph on each feature, supplying various testing scenarios and their expected output. Preferably, a full analysis would be done on the existing application, but in practice this can add considerable time and personnel to the effort, which may not be feasible and is rarely funded. A more realistic approach is to document the features in paragraph form, and create detailed requirements only for complex interactions that require detailed documentation.

  It is usually not enough to document only the user interface(s) of the current application. If the interface functionality doesn't show the intricacies of the underlying functional behavior inside the application and how such intricacies interact with the interface, this documentation will be insufficient.

- *Document updates to the existing application.* Updates—that is, additional or changed requirements—for the existing baseline application from this point forward should be documented for reference later, when the new application is ready to be upgraded. This will allow stable analysis of the existing functionality, and the creation of appropriate design and testing documents. If applicable, requirements, test procedures, and other test artifacts can be used for both products.

If updates are not documented, development of the new product will become "reactive": Inconsistencies between the legacy and new products will surface piecemeal; some will be corrected while others will not; and some will be known in advance while others will be discovered during testing or, worse, during production.

- *Implement an effective development process going forward.* Even though the legacy system may have been developed without requirements, design or test documentation, or any system-development processes, whenever a new feature is developed for either the previous or the new application, developers should make sure a system-development process has been defined, is communicated, is followed, and is adjusted as required, to avoid perpetuating bad software engineering practices.

After following these steps, the feature set of the application under development will have been outlined and quantified, allowing for better organization, planning, tracking, and testing of each feature.

CHAPTER 2
Test Planning

The cornerstone of a successful test program is effective test planning. Proper test planning requires an understanding of the corporate culture and its software-development processes, in order to adapt or suggest improvements to processes as necessary.

Planning must take place as early as possible in the software life cycle, because lead times must be considered for implementing the test program successfully. Gaining an understanding of the task at hand early on is essential in order to estimate required resources, as well as to get the necessary buy-in and approval to hire personnel and acquire testing tools, support software, and hardware. Early planning allows for testing schedules and budgets to be estimated, approved, and then incorporated into the overall software development plan.

Lead times for procurement and preparation of the testing environment, and for installation of the system under test, testing tools, databases, and other components must be considered early on.

No two testing efforts are the same. Effective test planning requires a clear understanding of all parts that can affect the testing goal. Additionally, experience and an understanding of the testing discipline are necessary, including best practices, testing processes, techniques, and tools, in order to select the test strategies that can be most effectively applied and adapted to the task at hand.

During test-strategy design, risks, resources, time, and budget constraints must be considered. An understanding of estimation techniques and their implementation is needed in order to estimate the required resources and functions, including number of personnel, types of expertise, roles and responsibilities, schedules, and budgets.

There are several ways to estimate testing efforts, including ratio methods and comparison to past efforts of similar scope. Proper estimation allows an effective test team to be assembled—not an easy task, if it must be done from scratch— and allows project delivery schedules to most accurately reflect the work of the testing team.

Item 6: Understand the Task At Hand and the Related Testing Goal

Testing, in general, is conducted to verify that software meets specific criteria and satisfies the requirements of the end user. Effective testing increases the probability that the application under test will function correctly under all circumstances and will meet the defined requirements, thus satisfying the end users of the application. Essential to achieving this goal is the detection and removal of defects in the software, whether through inspections, walk-throughs, testing, or excellent software development practices.

A program is said to function correctly when:

- Given valid input, the program produces the correct output as defined by the specifications.

- Given invalid input, the program correctly and gracefully rejects the input (and, if appropriate, displays an error message).

- The program doesn't hang or crash, given either valid or invalid input.

- The program keeps running correctly for as long as expected.

- The program achieves its functional and nonfunctional requirements. (For a discussion of nonfunctional requirements, see Chapter 9).

It is not possible to test all conceivable combinations and variations of input to verify that the application's functional and nonfunctional requirements have been met under every possible scenario.

Additionally, it is well known that testing alone cannot produce a quality product—it is not possible to "test quality into a product." Inspections, walk-throughs, and quality software engineering processes are all necessary to enhance the quality of a product.

Testing, however, may be seen as the final "quality gate."

Test strategies (see Item 7) must be defined that will help achieve the testing goal in the most effective manner. It is often not possible to fix all known defects and still meet the deadlines set for a project, so defects must be prioritized: It is neither necessary nor cost-effective to fix all defects before a release.

The specific test goal varies from one test effort to another, and from one test phase to the next. For example, the goal for testing a program's functionality is different from the goal for performance or configuration testing. The test planner, usually the test manager or test lead, must ask: What is the goal of the specific testing effort? This goal is based on criteria the system must meet.

Understanding the task at hand, its scope, and its associated testing goals are the first steps in test planning. Test planning requires a clear understanding of every piece that will play a part in achieving the testing goal.

How can the testing team gather this understanding? The first inclination of the test manager might be to take all of the documented requirements and develop a test plan, including a testing strategy, then break down the requirements feature-by-feature, and finally, task the testing team with designing and developing test procedures. However, without a broader knowledge of the task at hand, this is an ill-advised approach, since it is imperative that the testing team first understand all of the components that are a part of the testing goal. This is accomplished through the following:

- *Understanding the system.* The overall system view includes understanding of the functional and nonfunctional requirements (see Item 2) the system under test must meet. The testing team must understand these requirements to be effective. Reading a disjointed list of "The system shall..." statements in a requirements-specification document will hardly provide the necessary overall picture, because the scenarios and functional flow are often not apparent in such separate and isolated statements. Meetings involving overall system discussions, as well as documentation, should be made available to help provide the overall picture. Such documents would include proposals discussing the problem the proposed system is intended to solve. Other documents that can help further the understanding of the system may include statements of high-level business requirements, product management case studies, and business cases. For example, systems where there is no tolerance for error, such as medical devices where lives are at stake, will require a different approach than some business systems where there is a higher tolerance for error.

- *Early involvement.* The test manager, test lead, and other test-team members as necessary should be involved during the system's inception phase, when the first decisions about the system are made, in order to gain insights into tasks at hand. Such involvement adds to understanding of customer needs, issues, potential risks, and, most importantly, functionality.

- *Understanding corporate culture and processes.* Knowledge of the corporate culture and its software-development processes is necessary to adapt or suggest improvements as needed. Though every team member should be trying to improve the processes, in some organizations process improvement is the responsibility primary of QA and a Process Engineering Group.

  The test manager must understand the types of processes that are supported in order to be able to adapt a testing strategy that can achieve the defined goal. For example:

  - Does the testing effort involve a testing team independent from the development team, as opposed to having test engineers integrated with the development team?

  - Is an "extreme programming[1]" development effort underway, to which testing methods must be adapted?

  - Is the testing team the final quality gate—does the testing team give the green light regarding whether the testing criteria have been met?

- *Scope of Implementation.* In addition to comprehending the problem the system is intended to solve and the corporate culture, the team must understand the scope of the implementation in order to scale the testing scope accordingly.

- *Testing expectations.* What testing expectations does management have? What type of testing does the customer expect? For example, is a user-acceptance testing phase required? If so, which methodology must be followed, if any are specified, and what are the expected milestones and deliverables? What are the expected testing phases? Questions such as these are often answered in a project-management plan. The answers should all end up in the test plan.

---

1. For a description of extreme programming, see Item 29, Endnote 1.

- *Lessons learned.* Were any lessons learned from previous testing efforts? This is important information when determining strategies and for setting realistic expectations.

- *Level of effort.* What is the expected scale of the effort to build the proposed system? How many developers will be hired? This information will be useful for many purposes, such as projecting the complexity and scale of the testing effort, which can be based on a developer-to-tester ratio. See Item 12 for a discussion of test-effort estimation.

- *Type of solution.* Will the ultimate, most complex solution be implemented, or a more cost-effective solution that requires less development time? Knowing this will help the test planner understand the type of testing required.

- *Technology choices.* What technologies have been selected for the system's implementation, and what are the potential issues associated with them? What kind of architecture will the system use? Is it a desktop application, a client-server application, or a Web application? This information will help in determining test strategies and choosing testing tools.

- *Budget.* What is the budget for implementing this product or system, including testing? This information will be helpful in determining the types of testing possible given the level of funding. Unfortunately, budgets are often determined without any real effort at estimating testing costs, requiring the test manager to adapt the testing effort to fit a predetermined budget figure.

- *Schedule.* How much time has been allocated for developing and testing the system? What are the deadlines? Unfortunately, schedules too often are determined without any real test-schedule estimation effort, requiring the test manager to adapt a testing schedule to the fit a predetermined deadline.

- *Phased solution.* Does the implementation consist of a **phased** solution, with many releases containing incremental additions of functionality, or will there be one big release? If the release is phased, the phases and priorities must be understood so test development can be matched to the phases and implemented according to the iterations.

A broad understanding of what the system-to-be is to accomplish, its size and the corresponding effort involved, customer issues, and potential risks allows the test manager to comprehend the testing task at hand and architect the testing goal and its associated testing framework, eventually to be documented and communicated in a test plan or test-strategy document.

In addition, lead time is required to determine budgets and schedules and to meet other needs, such as procuring hardware and software required for the test environment, and evaluating, purchasing, and implementing a testing tool. The earlier the need for a test tool can be established, the better the chances that the correct tool can be acquired and applied effectively.

Item 7: Consider the Risks

Test-program **assumptions**, **prerequisites**, and **risks** must be understood before an effective testing strategy can be developed. This includes any events, actions, or circumstances that may prevent the test program from being implemented or executed according to schedule, such as late budget approvals, delayed arrival of test equipment, or late availability of the software application.

Test strategies include very specific activities that must be performed by the test team in order to achieve a specific goal. Many factors must be considered when developing test strategies. For example, if the application's architecture consists of several tiers, they must be considered when devising the testing strategy.

Test strategies generally must incorporate ways to minimize the risk of cost overruns, schedule slippage, critical software errors, and other failures. During test-strategy design, constraints on the task at hand (see Item 6), including risks, resources, time limits, and budget restrictions, must be considered.

A test strategy is best determined by narrowing down the testing tasks as follows:

- *Understand the system architecture.* Break down the system into its individual layers, such as user interface or database access. Understanding the architecture will help testers define the testing strategy for each layer or combination of layers and components. For further discussion of the system architecture, see Chapter 4.

- *Determine whether to apply GUI testing, back-end testing, or both.* Once the system architecture is understood, it can be determined how best to approach the testing—through the Graphical User Interface (GUI), against the back-end, or both. Most testing efforts will require that testing be applied at both levels, as the GUI often contains code that must be exercised and verified.

When determining the testing strategy, testers should keep in mind that the overall complexity of, and degree of expertise required for, business-layer (back-end) testing is much greater than for user-interface testing employed on the front-end parts of the application. This is because more complex language and technology skills are required to write tests that access the business layer— for example, self-sufficient, experienced C++ programmers may be needed if the business layer is written in C++. GUI tools and GUI testing, on the other hand, do not require extensive programming background; general programming skills or subject matter expertise (depending on the type of tester) may be the main requirements.

When determining the type of testing strategy to deploy, testers should consider at what point additional testing yields diminishing returns. For example, suppose an application is being developed for which GUI tests can successfully execute approximately 75% of the functionality, and approximately 25% can be tested using targeted business-layer tests (targeted at the highest-risk areas of the application) over the same period of time. It would not be necessary (or reasonable) to test the remaining 75% of the business layer. The effort would require a much higher number of skilled development resources, increase costs, and probably consume more time. It would be excessive and unnecessary to perform low-level testing on the remaining 75% because that functionality is exercised via the GUI, which will also have been tested.

Ideally, the GUI scripts will have been developed in such a manner that they rarely break. If not, then it may be necessary to perform further business-level testing.

The example of a 75:25 proportion of GUI to business-layer testing may require two GUI automaters and one business-layer test developer, in addition to several domain expert testers, who use manual techniques all depending on the size and complexity of the application. (For a discussion of Automated Testing, see Chapter 8.) In this example, five or more skilled C++ developers may be required to properly test the entire application at the business layer, depending on the number of layers, or logical tiers, in the application. They would need to work in lockstep with the development team, since the underlying business-layer interfaces can (and often do) change from build to build without affecting the GUI.

Low-level testing would not be necessary for the 75% of the application that follows straightforward record retrieval and record update models. However, GUI testing would still be required to make sure there are no data-handling issues or other minor flaws in the GUI itself.

The previous example demonstrates why it is important to apply testing strategies that make sense considering risk, complexity, and necessity. There is no hard-and-fast rule, however; each project requires its own individual analysis.

- *Select test-design techniques.* Narrowing down the types of testing techniques to be used can help reduce a large set of possible input combinations and variations. Various test-design techniques are available, and which to use must be determined as part of the testing strategy. Some test-design techniques are discussed in Chapter 5.

- *Select testing tools.* When developing the testing strategy, testers must determine the types of vendor-provided testing tools to be used, if any, given the testing task at hand; how the tools will be used; and which team members will be using them. It may also be necessary to build a tool instead of buying one. See Chapter 7 for a discussion of automated testing tools, including build-versus-buy decisions.

- *Develop in-house test harnesses or scripts.* The test designers may decide to develop an in-house automated test harness (see Item 37) or test tool, given the knowledge of the task at hand and the types of automated testing tools available on the market. When the testing task does not lend itself to a vendor-provided automated testing tool, in-house script and test harness development may be necessary.

- *Determine test personnel and expertise required.* Based on the test strategy outline, the required test personnel and expertise must be determined. If developing a test harness, a developer (i.e., a tester who has development skills) must be included on the testing team. If part of the testing strategy involves automation using capture/playback tools, automation skills will be required. Also needed is someone with domain expertise—knowledge in the subject matter to be tested. Not having the right skills in a testing team can significantly endanger the success of the testing effort. See Chapter 3 for a discussion of the testing team.

- *Determine testing coverage.* Testers must understand the testing coverage required. In some cases, for example, there may be contractual agreements that list all functional requirements to be tested, or code-coverage requirements. In other cases, testers must determine the testing coverage, given the resources, schedules, tools, task at hand, and risks of not testing an item. At the outset, testers should document what the testing will cover and what it won't.

- *Establish release criteria.* Stating the testing coverage is closely related to defining release or exit criteria. **Release criteria** indicate when testing can be considered complete, so it is important that they are documented upfront. For example, a release criterion might state that the application can ship with cosmetic defects, whereas all urgent and "show-stopper" defects must be fixed before release. Another release criterion might state that a certain high-priority feature must be working properly before the release can go out.

- *Set the testing schedule.* The testing strategy must be tailored to the time allotted to the testing effort. It's important that a detailed schedule be included in the testing strategy to avoid implementing a strategy that doesn't meet the required schedule.

- *Consider the testing phases.* Different test strategies apply to different testing phases. For example, during the functional testing phase, tests verify that the functional requirements have been met, while during the performance testing phase, performance tests verify that performance requirements have been met. Are there plans in place to have the system alpha tested or beta tested? Understanding the testing phases is necessary in order to develop adequate testing strategies for each phase.

These are just some of the issues to consider when developing a testing strategy. Since there is never enough time to test a system exhaustively, it is important to understand **project risks** when defining a testing strategy. Risk scenarios must be planned for, isolated to some degree, and managed. To this end, the test team must prioritize requirements and assess the risk inherent in each. The team must review the critical functions and high-risk elements identified for the system, and consider this information when determining the priority order of the test requirements.

When determining the order of test procedure development, the test team should review requirements to ensure that requirement areas have been prioritized, from most critical to least critical functionality, by the product-management or requirements team. Input from end users should have been considered in determining relative importance of functions. The prioritized requirements list should be made available to the testing team.

In addition to prioritizing areas of functionality, it is helpful to group requirements into related functional paths, scenarios, or flow. This makes it easier to assign test tasks to the various test engineers.

The criteria listed below for determining the order in which to group requirements are based on the recommendations of Rational Software Corporation.[1]

- *Risk level.* After risk assessment, test requirements are prioritized to ensure mitigation of high risks to system performance or the potential exposure of the company to liability. High-risk issues may include functions that prohibit data entry, for example, or business rules that could corrupt data or result in violation of regulations.

- *Operational characteristics.* Some test requirements will rank high on the priority list because they apply to frequently-used functions or are based upon a lack of knowledge of the user in the area. Functions pertaining to technical resources or internal users, and those that are infrequently used, are ranked lower in priority.

- *User requirements.* Some test requirements are vital to user acceptance. If the test approach does not emphasize the verification of these requirements, the resulting product may violate contractual obligations or expose the company to financial loss. It is important that the impact upon the end user of any potential problem be assessed.

- *Available resources.* A factor in the prioritization of test requirements is the availability of resources. As previously discussed, the test program must be designed in the context of constraints including limited staff availability, limited hardware availability, and conflicting project requirements. Here is where the painful process of weighing trade-offs is performed.

Most risk is caused by a few factors:

- *Short time-to-market.* A short time-to-market schedule for the software product makes availability of engineering resources all the more important. As

---

1. Rational Unified Process 5.0 (Rational Software Corporation, retrieved Sept. 7, 2002 from http://www.rational.com/products/rup/index.jsp).

previously mentioned, testing budgets and schedules are often determined at the onset of a project, during proposal development, without inputs from testing personnel, reference to past experience, or other effective estimation techniques. A good test manager can quickly ascertain when a short-time-to-market schedule would prevent adequate testing. Test strategies must be adapted to fit the time available. It is imperative that this issue be pointed out immediately so schedules can be adjusted, or the risks of fast development can be identified and risk-mitigation strategies developed.

- *New design processes.* Introduction of new design processes, including new design tools and techniques, increases risk.

- *New technology.* If new technology is implemented, there may be a significant risk that the technology will not work as expected, will be misunderstood and implemented incorrectly, or will require patches.

- *Complexity.* Analyses should be performed to determine which functionality is most complex and error-prone and where failure would have high impact. Test-team resources should be focused on these areas.

- *Frequency of use.* The potential failure of functionality that is used most often in an application (the "core" of the application) poses a high risk.

- *Untestable requirements.* Functional or nonfunctional requirements that cannot be tested pose a high risk to the success of the system. However, if the testing team has verified the testability of the requirements during the requirements phase (see Chapter 1), this issue may be minimized.

As risks are identified, they must be assessed for impact and then mitigated with strategies for overcoming them, because risks may be realized even though all precautions have been taken. The test team must carefully examine risks in order to derive effective test and mitigation strategies for a particular application.

Risk assessments must consider probability of a risk being realized and usage patterns that may cause the problem to appear, as well as mitigation strategies. The magnitude or impact of the potential problem should be evaluated. Risk mitigation strategies should be defined for those system requirements where there is the greatest probability of the risk being realized, balanced with amount of use and the importance of an area. Usually, the primary areas of an application should be allowed to contain few if any defects, while rarely used and less-important items may be allowed more latitude.

It is difficult to assess risk in great detail. A large number of people should contribute to this process, such as the customer representative (product management), end users, and the requirements, development, testing, and QA teams.

The degree of risk needs to be communicated so that decisions are informed ones. If the risk is too high, a recommendation can be made that the project not proceed in its current form, and be modified or discontinued altogether.

Risk analysis provides information that can assist the test manager or test-team lead in making difficult decisions such as assignment of testers based on skill level, effort to be expended, and risk and quality goals. After performance of a risk assessment in which a deliverable is determined to have high risk factors, and failure to deliver might have a strong negative impact, a decision may be made to assign experienced tester(s) to this area.

One testing strategy that helps mitigate risks is to focus the testing on the parts of the system that are likely to cause most of the problems. The test engineer or test manager must identify the parts of an implementation cycle that pose the greatest risk, and the functionality that most likely will cause problems or failures.

On the other hand, for a deliverable that has low risk factors and low impacts, inspections may cover all the testing necessary for this particular deliverable. Low-risk, low-impact deliverables can also provide opportunities for new or less experienced testers to gain practice with minimal risk.

Careful examination of goals and risks is necessary for development of an appropriate set of test strategies, which in turn produces a more predictable, higher-quality outcome.

Item 8: Base Testing Efforts on a Prioritized Feature Schedule

Software feature implementations must be prioritized for each incremental software release, based on customer needs or the necessity to deliver some high-risk items first. However, test-procedure planning and development should be based not only on priority and risk, as discussed in Item 7, but also on the software feature implementation schedule, as the latter dictates the order in which features are made available for testing.

It is important that the software development schedule, including the feature implementation sequence, is decided early and made available to the testing team so it can plan accordingly. This is especially true when time is limited, to avoid wasting time developing tests for features that won't be made available until later releases. Frequent changes to the feature schedule should be avoided, as each modification requires changes in development and testing plans and schedules.

Feature prioritization is especially crucial for phased releases. In most cases, the development schedule should strive to deliver the most needed features first. Those features, in turn, should be tested first.

Feature lists can be prioritized based on various criteria:

- *Highest to lowest risk.* As described in Item 7, it is important to consider levels of risk when developing a project schedule and the associated testing strategy. Focusing development and testing on the highest-risk features is one way to prioritize.

- *Highest to lowest complexity.* Prioritizing by complexity—attempting to develop and test the most complex features first—may minimize schedule overruns.

- *Customer needs.* For most projects, there is a tendency to prioritize feature delivery based on customer needs, since this is usually required to fuel the marketing and sales activities associated with a product.

- *Budget constraints.* The vast majority of software projects go over their budgets. It's important to consider the allotted testing budget when prioritizing the features for a given release. Some features will be more important to the success of a program than others.

- *Time constraints.* It's important to consider time constraints when prioritizing the features for a given release.

- *Personnel constraints.* When prioritizing the feature schedule, planners should consider availability of personnel. Key personnel required to implement a specific feature might be missing from the team because of budget constraints or other issues. While prioritizing features, it's important to consider not only "what" but "who."

A combination of several of these approaches is typically necessary to arrive at an effective feature schedule. Each feature can be given a "score" for risk, complexity, customer need, and so on to arrive at a total value, or "weight," for that feature. Once this is done for each feature, the list can be sorted by weight to arrive at a prioritized list of features.

Item 9: Keep Software Issues in Mind

When developing testing plans, it is important for the testing team to understand the software issues affecting project development and delivery. These include:

- *Beta or pre-release products.* The development team may be implementing new features on a beta version of a particular technology or operating system. When a development team is working with the beta version of some technology, chances are that no automated testing tool is available that specifically supports all of the beta technology. The test plan must take this into account, and must provide for evaluation of all technologies used by development team as early as possible in the life cycle to determine whether available testing tools will suffice.

- *New or cutting-edge technologies.* Implementation of new technologies inevitably causes disruptions in development, with the potential for ripple effects throughout many stages of the software development life cycle, including testing activities. Sometimes a new technology can present so many problems that it may be necessary to reengineer a portion of the product. For example, suppose the development group has implemented a solution using the beta version of an operating system, but when the release version becomes available, it has been rearchitected in such a way that it requires the development team to reengineer parts of the implementation. This, in turn, requires the testing team to run another detailed regression test, to modify its gray-box[1] testing efforts, and forces

---

1. Gray-box testing exercises the application, either though the user interface or directly against the underlying components, while monitoring internal component behavior to determine the success or failure of the test. See Item 16.

the testing team to redevelop automated testing scripts that had already been created. Issues such as these must be considered during test planning.

- *Staged implementation.* Prior to completion of the initial version of a system, functionality becomes available in pieces. Testing must be coordinated with feature delivery. For example, the application may provide a user interface for entering a set of data, but the interface for viewing that data may not be available until much later. The test plan must accommodate such conditions by providing alternative ways of testing whether the application correctly processes and stores the data.

- *Defects.* Defects may prevent testing from proceeding in numerous areas. It may be impossible for test procedures to be executed in their entirety: The system may fail prior to the execution of all test steps. This is especially true during the early phases of software construction, when the number of defects is high. To properly handle this situation, it is necessary to communicate to the development team that defects are preventing testing from continuing, so repairing these defects can be accorded higher priority.

- *Patches and service packs.* Operating system vendors and other third-party software suppliers often provide updates to correct problems and introduce new features. If the application under test will be affected by such updates, it is important to factor this into the test plan. For example, when a new version of a popular Web browser is released, many users will upgrade to this new version. The test plan must make provisions for acquiring the new browser as soon as possible and testing the compatibility of the application with this browser, as well as with older versions. Similarly, when an operating system service pack is released, many users will install the service pack. The application must be tested for compatibility with this update as soon as possible. Testers should not rely upon assurance that a service pack is supposed to be backward compatible.

Item 10: Acquire Effective Test Data

D uring the creation of detailed test designs (discussed in Chapter 5), test data requirements are incorporated into test cases, which in turn are part of the test procedures.[1] An effective test strategy requires careful acquisition and preparation of test data. Functional testing can suffer if test data is poor. Conversely, good data can help improve functional testing. Good test data can be structured to improve understanding and testability. Its contents, correctly chosen, can reduce maintenance effort. When requirements are vague, preparation of high-quality test data can help to focus the business.

A good **data dictionary** and detailed **design documentation** can be useful in developing sample data. In addition to providing data-element names, the data dictionary may describe data structures, cardinality, usage rules, and other useful information. Design documentation, particularly database schemas, can also help identify how the application interacts with data as well as relationships between data elements.

Given the sheer number of possibilities, it is usually not possible to test all possible combinations and variations of inputs and outputs to verify that the application's functional and nonfunctional requirements have been met under every conceivable condition. However, various test-design techniques are available to help narrow down the data input and output combinations and variations. One such test technique is **data flow coverage**. It is designed to incorporate the flow of data into the selection of test-procedure steps, helping to identify test paths that satisfy some characteristic of data flow for all applicable paths.

---

1. Per ANSI/IEEE Standard 829-1987, test design identifies the test cases, which contain the test data.

Boundary-condition testing is another testing technique. Test data is prepared that executes each **boundary condition** (limit on quantity or content of allowable data, set in the software design). The behavior of systems usually changes at their boundaries. Errors congregate at the boundaries; therefore, testing system behavior at these boundaries is a very effective technique.

Boundary conditions should be listed in the requirement statements—for example, "the system will support a range of 1 to 100 items in a pick-list control." In this example, the boundary conditions tested could be 100+1 (outside the boundary), 100-1 (inside the boundary), 100 (on the boundary); and 1 (on the boundary), null (no input), and 0 (outside the boundary). When boundary conditions are not specified in the system requirements, the test plan must incorporate tests that actually find the boundaries. These types of tests are very common, since developers often don't know the boundaries until they are determined via focused testing.

Ideally, such issues would have been resolved while determining the testability of the requirements. Given the complexity of today's technologies, however, determining system boundaries during the requirements phase often is not possible. One alternative way to do so is to develop and test a prototype of the software.

Test data must be designed to allow each system-level requirement to be tested and verified. A review of test-data requirements should address several data concerns, including those listed below.[2]

- *Depth.* The test team must consider the quantity and size of database records needed to support tests. The test team must identify whether 10 records within a database or particular table are sufficient, or 10,000 records are necessary. Early life-cycle tests, such as unit or build verification, should use small, hand-crafted databases, which offer maximum control and the most-focused effort. As the test effort progresses through the different phases and types of tests, the size of the database should increase as appropriate for particular tests. For example, performance and volume tests are not meaningful if the production environment database contains 1,000,000 records, but tests are performed against a database containing only 100 records. For additional discussion on performance testing and the importance that it be done early in the development lifecycle, see Chapter 9.

---

2. Adapted from the SQA Suite Process, Rational Unified Process 5.0 in Ivar Jacobson, Grady Booch, and James Rumbaugh, *The Unified Software Development Process* (Reading, Mass.: Addison-Wesley, Feb. 1999).

- *Breadth.* Test engineers must investigate variations within the data values (e.g., 10,000 different accounts containing different data values, and a number of different types of accounts containing different *types* of data). A well-designed test will account for variations in test data, whereas tests for which all the data is similar will produce limited results.

   With regard to records containing different data *values,* testers may need to consider, for example, that some accounts may have negative balances, or balances in the low range (e.g., $100s), moderate range ($1,000s), high range ($100,000s), and very high range ($10,000,000s). With regard to records containing different data *types,* testers must consider, for example, bank customer accounts that might be classified in several ways, including savings, checking, loans, student, joint, and business accounts.

- *Scope.* The scope of test data is pertinent to the accuracy, relevance, and completeness of the data. For example, when testing queries used to identify the various kinds of accounts at a bank that have balance-due amounts greater than $100, not only should there be numerous accounts in the test data that meet this criterion, but the tests must also reflect additional data, such as reason codes, contact histories, and account owner demographic data. The use of complete test data enables the test procedure to fully validate and exercise the system and to support the evaluation of results. The test engineer must also verify that the inclusion of a record returned as a result of a query (e.g., accounts with balance-due amounts greater than $100) is valid for the specific purpose of the query, and not due to a missing or inappropriate value.

- *Data integrity during test execution.* The test team must maintain data integrity while performing tests. The test team must be able to segregate data, modify selected data, and return the database to its initial state throughout test operations. The test team must make sure that when several test engineers are performing tests at the same time, one test won't adversely affect the data required for the other tests. For example, if one test team member is modifying data values while another is running a query, the result of the query may not be as expected. One way to prevent one tester's work from interfering with another's is to assign a separate test database or data file to each tester, if feasible and cost-effective. Another way is to assign separate testing tasks to each tester, focusing each on a specific area of functionality that does not overlap with others being tested.

- *Conditions.* Data sets should be created that reflect specific "conditions" in the domain of the application, meaning certain patterns of data that would otherwise be arrived at only after performing specific operations over time. For example, financial systems commonly perform year-end closeouts. Storing data in the year-end condition enables the system to be tested in a year-end closeout state without having to first enter the data for the entire year. Creating test data that is already in the closeout state eases testing, since testers can simply load the closeout test data without having to perform many operations to get data into the closeout state.

When identifying test-data requirements, it is beneficial to develop a table listing the test procedures in one column and test-data requirements in another column. Among the requirements, it is important to note the size of the data set needed, and how long it will take to generate the test data. While a small data subset is good enough for functional testing, a production-sized database is required for performance testing. It can take a long time to acquire production-size data, sometimes as long as several months.

The test team also must plan the means for obtaining, generating, or developing the test data. The mechanism for refreshing the test database to an original state, to enable all testing activities including regression testing, also must be devised and documented in the project test plan. Testers must identify the names and locations of the applicable test databases and repositories necessary to exercise and test the software application.

Data usually must be prepared prior to testing. **Data preparation** may involve the processing of raw data text, or files; consistency checks; and in-depth analysis of data elements, including defining data to test case-mapping criteria, clarifying data-element definitions, confirming primary keys, and defining acceptable data parameters. In order to prepare the data, as well as to develop environment setup scripts and test-bed scripts, the test team must obtain and modify all needed test databases. Ideally, existing customer data is available that includes realistic combinations and variations of data scenarios. An advantage of using actual customer data is that it may include some combinations or usage patterns that had not been considered by test designers. Having actual customer data available during testing can be a useful reality check for the application.

Item 11: Plan the Test Environment

The **test environment** comprises all of the elements that support the physical testing effort, such as test data, hardware, software, networks, and facilities. Test-environment plans must identify the number and types of individuals who require access to the test environment, and specify a sufficient number of computers to accommodate these individuals. (For a discussion of test-team membership, see Chapter 3.) Consideration should be given to the number and kinds of environment-setup scripts and test-bed scripts that will be required.

In this chapter, the term **production environment** refers to the environment in which the final software will run. This could range from a single end-user computer to a network of computers connected to the Internet and serving a complete Web site.

While unit- and integration-level tests are usually performed within the development environment by the development staff, system tests and user-acceptance tests are ideally performed within a separate test-lab setting that represents a configuration identical to the production environment, or at least a scaled-down version of the production environment. The test-environment configuration must be representative of the production environment because the test environment must be able to replicate the baseline configuration of the production environment in order to uncover any configuration-related issues that may affect the application, such as software incompatibilities, clustering, and firewall issues. However, fully replicating the production environment is often not feasible, due to cost and resource constraints.

After gathering and documenting the facts as described above, the test team must compile the following information and resources preparatory to designing a test environment:

- Obtain descriptions of sample customer environments, including a listing of support software, COTS (commercial off-the-shelf) tools, computer hardware and operating systems. Hardware descriptions should include such elements as video resolution, hard-disk space, processing speed, and memory characteristics, as well as printer characteristics including type of printer, capacity, and whether the printer is dedicated to the user's machine or connected to a network server.

- Determine whether the test environment requires an archive mechanism, such as a tape drive or recordable CD (CD-R) drive, to allow the storage of large files (especially log files on client-server systems) post-test. Archiving is almost a necessity in current testing environments.

- Identify network characteristics of the customer environment, such as the use of leased lines, modems, Internet connections, and protocols such as Ethernet, IPX, and TCP/IP.

- In the case of a client-server or Web-based system, identify the required server operating systems, databases, and other components.

- Identify the number of automated test tool-licenses required by the test team.

- Identify other software needed to execute certain test procedures, such as word processors, spreadsheets, and report writers.

- When specifying test-environment hardware, consider test-data requirements, including the size of the test databases if applicable. It is important to ensure that the machines possess sufficient capacity and that resources needed to install the data, such as a tape drive or network connection, are available.

- Consider special resources needed for configuration testing, such as removable hard drives and image-retrieval software.

Following these preparatory activities, the test team develops a test-environment design that consists of a graphic representation of the test-environment architecture, together with a list of the components required to support that architecture. The list of components must be reviewed to determine which components are already in place, which can be shifted from other locations within the organization, and which must be procured. The list of components that must be procured comprises a **test equipment purchase list**. It enumerates quantities required, unit price information, and maintenance and support costs. The test team may want to include a few backup components, in order to ensure that testing can continue in the event of hardware failure.

Item 12: Estimate Test Preparation and Execution Time[1]

B efore it is possible to complete that ideal test plan and the best testing strategy, it is necessary to estimate how long it will take to prepare and execute the tests. It is important to remember to include testing time estimates when scoping out the overall software development schedule.

Historically, development and overall project effort have been the predominant focus of software development program estimation. The time required for product quality assurance disciplines, such as software testing, has often been loosely estimated in relation to the amount of anticipated development effort or overall project effort. However, because of variability in testing protocols, it is usually insufficient to estimate testing time in this way; a variety of factors that will affect a particular testing effort must be taken into account.

The test effort applied to a particular project depends on a number of variables. These include the culture or "test maturity" of the organization, the complexity of the software application under test, the scope of test requirements defined for the project, the skill levels of the individuals performing the tests, and the type of test-team organization supporting the test effort. These variables can be used as inputs into complex models supported by automated estimation tools in order to develop test-team resource estimates.

However, given the large number of variables that affect the magnitude of the test effort, the use of complex equations is not generally useful, as estimation formulas are

---

1. Elfriede Dustin *et al.*, *Automated Software Testing* (Reading, Mass.: Addison-Wesley, 1999), Section 5.3.

rarely precise.[2] Such methods of projecting the level of effort for a test program do not normally produce an outcome that reflects the actual amount of effort that applies. Moreover, they are too cumbersome. Simpler estimation models, on the other hand, can serve well.

Ideally, test estimation should always begin with either a **work breakdown structure** (WBS) or a detailed list of testing tasks from which a "testing WBS" can be built.

To be most effective, the methods presented here must be adapted to the organization's needs and processes.

DEVELOPMENT RATIO METHOD

Given the predominant focus within the industry on estimating software development efforts, the exercise of sizing a test program is commonly based on the Development Ratio Method. This quick and easy way to gauge the level of effort required for a test program is centered upon the number of software developers planned for the effort. The size of the test team is calculated using the ratio of developers to test engineers on a project. The term **developers** in this case includes personnel dedicated to performing design-, development-, and unit-level test activities.

The result derived from this ratio depends on the type of software development effort, as shown in Table 12.1. The ratios in Table 12.1 are applicable when the scope of the test effort involves functional and performance testing at the integration and system test levels. Note that the ratio of test team members to developers depends on the type and complexity of software being developed. For example, when a commercial vendor creates software intended for a large worldwide audience, the emphasis on testing increases, so the ratio of test engineers to developers increases. A test effort for a software product with a smaller market requires a lower ratio of test engineers to developers, all other factors being equal.

Additionally, at different times during the development life-cycle, the ratio may change. During the later testing phases, when schedules are tight and deadlines are near, developers, temps, and product management members might be assigned to help with testing. At such times, the ratio of testers to developers will increase, and the number of testers may even exceed the number of developers.

---

2. For more information on this topic, see J.P. Lewis, "Large Limits to Software Estimation," *ACM Software Engineering Notes* 26:4 (July, 2001): 54–59.

During test planning, the projected ratios must be seen as approximations or ideals. The ratios actually implemented will vary based on available budget, buy-in of decision makers to the testing effort, complexity of the application, test effectiveness, and many more factors.

Table 12.1. Test-Team Size Calculated Using the Development-Ratio Method [a]

Product Type	Number of Developers	Ratio of Developers to Testers	Number of Testers
Commercial Product (Large Market)	30	3:2	20
Commercial Product (Small Market)	30	3:1	10
Development & Heavy COTS Integration for Individual Client	30	4:1	7
Government (Internal) Application Development	30	5:1	6
Corporate (Internal) Application Development	30	4:1	7

a. Ratios will differ depending on system complexity or when building systems where there is no tolerance for error, such as medical device systems or air traffic control systems.

PROJECT STAFF RATIO METHOD

Another quick way to estimate the number of personnel required to support a test program is to use the Project Staff Ratio method, as detailed in Table 12.2. This method is based on historical metrics, and uses the number of people planned to support an entire project—including requirements, configuration, process, development, and QA—to calculate the size of the test team. This method may be especially valuable when the number of people performing development work changes frequently or is difficult to quantify. In calculating the test-team sizes for Table 12.2, it is assumed that the scope of the test effort will include requirements reviews, configuration testing, process involvement, and functional and performance testing at the integration and system test levels. A baseline value of 50 in the "Project Staffing Level" column is selected to simplify calculation of the associated values in the "Test Team Size" column. The number of personnel on a project, of course, may be more or fewer.

Table 12.2. Test-Team Size Calculated Using the Project Staff Ratio Method

Development Type	Project Staffing Level	Test Team Size Factor	Number of Testers
Commercial Product (Large Market)	50	27%	13
Commercial Product (Small Market)	50	16%	8
Application Development for Individual Client	50	10%	5
Development & Heavy COTS Integration for Individual Client	50	14%	7
Government (Internal) Application Development	50	11%	5
Corporate (Internal) Application Development	50	14%	7

TEST PROCEDURE METHOD

Another way to estimate the level of effort required to support a test program is to use test program sizing estimates, in the form of the number of test procedures planned for a project. This method is somewhat limited because it focuses solely on the number of test procedures to be developed and executed, ignoring other important factors that affect the scale of the testing effort. To get a more comprehensive metric, this method must be used in combination with one of the other methods listed here.

To employ the Test Procedure Method, the organization must first develop a historical record of the various development projects that have been performed, with associated development sizing values such as function points, number of test procedures used, and the resulting test effort measured in terms of personnel hours. Development sizing values may be documented in terms of lines of code (LOC), lines of code equivalent, function points, or number of objects produced.

The test team then determines requirements and the relationship between historical development sizing values and the numbers of test procedures used in those projects, and calculates an estimate for the number of test procedures required for the new project. Next, the test team determines the historical relationship between number of test procedures and number of tester hours expended, taking into account experience from similar historical projects. The result is then used to estimate the number of personnel hours (or full time equivalent personnel) needed to support the test effort on the new project.

For this estimation method to be most successful, the projects being compared must be similar in nature, technology, required expertise, problems solved, and other factors, as described in the section titled "Other Considerations" later in this Item.

Table 12.3 shows example figures derived using the Test Procedure Method, where a test team has estimated that a new project will require 1,120 test procedures. The test team reviews historical records of test efforts on two or more similar projects, which on average involved 860 test procedures and required 5,300 personnel-hours for testing. In these previous test efforts, the number hours per test procedure was approximately 6.16 over the entire life cycle of testing activities, from startup and planning to design and development to test execution and reporting. The 5,300 hours were expended over an average nine-month period, representing 3.4 full-time-equivalent test engineers for the project. For the new project, the team plans to develop 1,120 test procedures.

Table 12.3. Test-Team Size Calculated Using the Test-Procedure Method

	Number of Test Procedures	Factor	Number of Person Hours	Performance Period	Number of Testers
Historical Record (Average of Two or More Similar Projects)	860	6.16	5,300	9 months (1,560 hrs)	3.4
New Project Estimate	1,120	6.16	6,900	12 months (2,080 hrs)	3.3

The factor derived using the Test Procedure Method is most reliable when the historical values are derived from projects undertaken after the testing culture of the organization has reached maturity.

It is also important to take into account the relationship between the number of test procedures applied to a project and the scope of test requirements. Successful employment of this method requires that the requirements and scope of the project have been defined beforehand. Unfortunately, test estimates often are requested, and needed, well before requirements have been finalized.

TASK PLANNING METHOD

Another way to estimate a test program's required level of effort involves the review of historical records with regard to the number of personnel hours expended to perform testing for a similar type of test effort. This method differs from the Test Procedure Method in that it focuses on testing *tasks*. Both methods require a highly structured environment in which various details are tracked and measured, such as the factors described under "Other Considerations" later in this Item. Earlier test efforts would need to have included time recording in accordance with a work-breakdown structure, so that historical records document the effort required to perform the various tasks.

In Table 12.4, an example new project estimated to require 1,120 test procedures is compared against a historical baseline. The historical record indicates that an average project involving 860 test procedures required 5,300 personnel hours, a factor of 6.16. This factor is used to estimate the number of hours required to perform 1,120 test procedures. (This is the same historical comparison used for the Test Procedure Method, reflected in Table 12.3.)

Table 12.4. Test-Personnel Hours Calculated Using the Task-Planning Method

	Number of Test Procedures	Factor	Test-Personnel Hours
Historical Record (Similar Project)	860	6.16	5,300
New Project Estimate	1,120	6.16	6,900

The test team then reviews the historical record to break out the hours expended on the various test program tasks within the test phases. A summary of hours for each phase is depicted in Table 12.5.

Table 12.5. Hours Expended in Each Testing Phase, Task-Planning Method

Phase	Historical Value	% of Project	Preliminary Estimate	Adjusted Estimate
1 Project Startup	140	2.6	179	179
2 Early Project Support (requirements analysis, etc.)	120	2.2	152	152
3 Decision to Automate Testing	90	1.7	117	-
4 Test Tool Selection and Evaluation	160	3	207	-
5 Test Tool Introduction	260	5	345	345
6 Test Planning	530	10	690	690
7 Test Design	540	10	690	690
8 Test Development	1,980	37	2,553	2,553
9 Test Execution	870	17	1,173	1,173
10 Test Management and Support	470	9	621	621
11 Test Process Improvement	140	2.5	173	-
PROJECT TOTAL	**5,300**	**100%**	**6,900**	**6,403**

To derive these figures, the test team first develops a preliminary estimate of the hours required for each phase, using the historical percentage factor. (If no historical data is available, it may be necessary to base these estimates on testers' past experience.) The right-hand column is for revisions as conditions change. In the example, the new project is mandated to use a particular automated testing tool, making Steps 3 and 4 superfluous. The test team is also advised that the project will not be provided any funding to cover test process improvement activities. The hours for Step 11 are therefore deleted in the revised estimate.

The next step, depicted in Table 12.6, is to compute the test-team size based on the adjusted personnel-hour estimate of 6,403 hours. The test team size is calculated to be equivalent to 3.1 test engineers over the twelve-month project. In the event that the test team is staffed with exactly three full time test personnel throughout the duration of the test effort, the team must achieve a slightly higher level of productivity than that of previous test teams in order to perform the test effort within the given schedule, if that is possible. More likely, the team must focus initially on only high risk items, while lower risk items will have to be addressed later on. The testing strategy must be adjusted accordingly, and reasons for the adjustment, such as not enough personnel, must be communicated.

The test team could implement a different staffing approach, which applies two full time test personnel plus the fractional time of two other test engineers. The fractional time could be split a number of ways, including 80% of one person and 80% of a second person.

Table 12.6. Test-Team Size Based on Personnel-Hour Estimate

	Number of Test Procedures	Personnel-Hour Estimate	Adjusted Estimate	Performance Period	Number of Testers
New Project Estimate	1,120	5.71	6,403	12 months (2,080 hrs)	3.1

OTHER CONSIDERATIONS

Regardless of the estimation method selected, experienced test professionals should consider any unusual circumstances that may operate against relying completely on projections from past testing efforts. For example, when using the Development Ratio Method in an organization that has not emphasized testing in the past—and therefore has not yet defined mature testing processes—it may be necessary to adjust the ratios accordingly. Similarly, when using the Task Planning Method, if the test team has recently experienced significant turnover, it may be prudent to adjust the factor derived. Issues to consider when estimating test efforts include the following:

- *Organization.* Test culture or test maturity of the organization.

- *Scope of test requirements.* Tests that must be performed can include functional-requirement testing, server-performance testing, user-interface testing, program module performance testing, program module complexity analysis, program code coverage testing, system load performance testing, boundary testing, security testing, memory-leak testing, response time performance testing, and usability testing, among others.

- *Test-engineer skill level.* Technical skill level of the individuals performing test.

- *Test-tool proficiency.* The use of automated testing introduces a new level of complexity that a project's test team may not have previously experienced. Tools require a learning curve. Test-script programming expertise is required. This may be new to the test team, and the team may lack experience in writing code. Even if the test team has experience with one kind of automated test tool, a different tool may be required on the new project.

- *Business knowledge.* Test-team personnel's familiarity with the application business area, also called "domain knowledge."

- *Test-team organization.* The test-team's organizational type can be a factor, since some team structures are more effective than others.[3]

- *Scope of test program.* An effective automated test program amounts to a development effort in itself, complete with strategy and goal planning, test-requirement definition, analysis, design, and coding.

- *Start of test effort.* Test planning and activity should begin early in the project. This means that test engineers must be involved in analysis and design review activities in order to prevent analysis and design errors. Early involvement allows the test team to more completely understand requirements and design, to architect the most appropriate test environment, and to generate a more thorough test design. Early involvement not only supports effective test design, which is critical especially when utilizing an automated test tool, but also provides opportunities for early detection of errors and

---

3. See Dustin *et al.*, *Automated Software Testing*, Chapter 5 for more information on test-team organization types.

prevents migration of errors from requirement specification to design, and from design into code.

- *Number of incremental software builds planned.* Many industry software professionals have a perception that the use of automated test tools makes the software test effort less significant in terms of personnel hours, or less complex in terms of planning and execution. Savings from the use of automated test tools will take time to accrue. In fact, at the first use of a particular automated test tool by a test team, very little savings may be realized. Savings are realized in subsequent builds of a software application.

- *Process definition.* Using defined (documented) processes improves efficiency in test-engineering operations. Lack of defined processes has the opposite effect, translating to longer learning curves for junior test engineers.

- *High-risk applications.* The scope and breadth of testing on software applications where a software failure poses a risk to human life is greater than for software applications that do not pose such high risks.

Insufficient time for test development and execution may lead to inefficiency in test-engineering operations and require additional test engineering to correct errors or oversights.

While the test effort required to support a software application project depends on a wide variety of variables, several simple, common methods of test effort estimation work well. This is because these simplified estimation methods reflect the standardized distribution of the effects of all these influences over time on the test effort.

The Development Ratio Method, which uses the size of the development team to determine the appropriate size for the test team, is perhaps the most common method of test-effort estimation. The Project Staff Ratio Method, which calculates test-team size based on overall project size, is generally the easiest way to determine the size of the test team. The Test Procedure and Task Planning methods require the maintenance of historical records in order to produce a sizing estimate based on the actual experience of an organization.

Finally, when sizing a test effort, it is important to review the list of test-effort sizing factors in order to consider unusual circumstances.

To assist in future planning, it is often useful to track actual team hours per task on the current project. This data can be quite useful in future test-team sizing efforts. However, the problem with all the methods provided is that rarely are any two software development projects alike. Complexity, developer's experience, technology, and numerous other variables change with most projects.

CHAPTER 3

The Testing Team

T he capabilities of the testing team can greatly affect the success, or failure, of
the testing effort. An effective testing team includes a mixture of technical and
domain expertise relevant to the software problem at hand. It is not enough
for a testing team to be technically proficient with the testing techniques and tools
necessary to perform the actual tests. Depending on the complexity of the domain, a
test team should also include members who have a detailed understanding of the
problem domain. This knowledge enables them to create effective test artifacts and
data and to effectively implement test scripts and other test mechanisms.

In addition, the testing team must be properly structured, with defined roles
and responsibilities that allow the testers to perform their functions with minimal overlap and without uncertainty regarding which team member should perform which duties. One way to divide testing resources is by specialization in
particular application areas and nonfunctional areas. The testing team may also
have more role requirements than it has members, which must be considered by
the test manager.

As with any team, continual evaluation of the effectiveness of each test team
member is important to ensuring a successful test effort. Evaluation of testers is performed by examining a variety of areas, including the types of defects generated, and
the number and types of defects missed. It is never good practice to evaluate a test
engineer's performance using numbers of defects generated alone, since this metric
by itself does not tell the whole story. Many factors must be considered during this
type of evaluation, such as complexity of functionality tested, time constraints, test

engineer role and responsibilities, experience, and so on. Regularly evaluating team members using valid criteria makes it possible to implement improvements that increase the effectiveness of the overall effort.

Item 13: Define Roles and Responsibilities[1]

Test efforts are complex, and require that the test team possess a diversity of expertise to comprehend the scope and depth of the required test effort and develop a strategy for the test program.

In order for everyone on the test team to be aware of what needs to get done and who will take the lead on each task, it is necessary to define and document the roles and responsibilities of the test-team members. These should be communicated, both verbally and in writing, to everyone on the team. Identifying the assigned roles of all test-team members on the project enables everyone to clearly understand which individual is responsible for each area of the project. In particular, it allows new team members to quickly determine whom to contact if an issue arises.

In order to identify the individuals needed to perform a particular task, a task description should be created. Once the scope of the task is understood, it will be easier to assign particular team members to the task.

To help ensure successful execution of the task, **work packages** can be developed and distributed to the members of the test team. Work packages typically include the organization of the tasks, technical approach, task schedule, spending plan, allocation of hours for each individual, and a list of applicable standards and processes.

The number of test-engineering roles in a project may be greater than the number of test-team members. (The roles required depend on the task at hand, as discussed

---

1. Adapted from Elfriede Dustin et al., *Automated Software Testing* (Reading, Mass.: Addison-Wesley, 1999), Table 5.11, 183–186.

in Chapter 2.) As a result, a test engineer may "wear many hats," being responsible for more than one role.

Table 13.1 shows some example responsibilities and skills required for each test-program role.

Table 13.1—Test Program Roles

Test Manager

Responsibilities	Skills
▪ Liaison for interdepartmental interactions: Representative of the testing team ▪ Customer interaction, if applicable ▪ Recruiting, staff supervision, and staff training ▪ Test budgeting and scheduling, including test-effort estimations	▪ Understands testing process or methodology ▪ Familiar with test-program concerns including test environment and data management, trouble reporting and resolution, and test design and development ▪ Understands manual testing techniques and automated testing best practices
▪ Test planning, including development of testing goals and strategy ▪ Vendor interaction ▪ Test-tool selection and introduction	▪ Understands application business area, application requirements
▪ Cohesive integration of test and development activities	▪ Skilled at developing test goals, objectives, and strategy
▪ Acquisition of hardware and software for test environment	▪ Familiar with different test tools, defect-tracking tools, and other test-support COTS tools and their use
▪ Test environment and test product configuration management.	▪ Good at all planning aspects, including people, facilities, and schedule
▪ Test-process definition, training and continual improvement	
▪ Use of metrics to support continual test-process improvement	
▪ Test-program oversight and progress tracking	
▪ Coordinating pre- and post-test meetings	

Test Lead

Responsibilities	Skills
▪ Technical leadership for the test program, including test approach	▪ Understands application business area and application requirements
▪ Support for customer interface, recruiting, test-tool introduction, test planning, staff supervision, and cost and progress status reporting	▪ Familiar with test-program concerns including test-data management, trouble reporting and resolution, test design, and test development
▪ Verifying the quality of the requirements, including testability, requirement definition, test design, test-script and test-data development, test automation, test-environment configuration; test-script configuration management, and test execution	▪ Expertise in a variety of technical skills including programming languages, database technologies, and computer operating systems
▪ Interaction with test-tool vendor to identify best ways to leverage test tool on the project	▪ Familiar with different test tools, defect-tracking tools, and other COTS tools supporting the testing life cycle, and their use
▪ Staying current on latest test approaches and tools, and transferring this knowledge to test team	
▪ Conducting test-design and test-procedure walk-throughs and inspections	
▪ Implementing test-process improvements resulting from lessons learned and benefits surveys	
▪ Test Traceability Matrix (tracing the test procedures to the test requirements)	
▪ Test-process implementation	
▪ Ensuring that test-product documentation is complete	

Usability[2] Test Engineer

Responsibilities	Skills
▪ Designs and develops usability testing scenarios ▪ Administers usability testing process	▪ Proficient in designing test suites ▪ Understanding usability issues
▪ Defines criteria for performing usability testing, analyzes results of testing sessions, presents results to development team	▪ Skilled in test facilitation
▪ Develops test-product documentation and reports	▪ Excellent interpersonal skills
▪ Defines usability requirements, and interacts with customer to refine them	▪ Proficient in GUI design standards
▪ Participates in test-procedure walk-throughs	

Manual Test Engineer

Responsibilities	Skills
▪ Designs and develops test procedures and cases, with associated test data, based upon functional and nonfunctional requirements	▪ Has good understanding of GUI design
▪ Manually executes the test procedures	▪ Proficient in software testing
▪ Attends test-procedure walk-throughs	▪ Proficient in designing test suites
▪ Conducts tests and prepares reports on test progress and regression	▪ Proficient in the business area of application under test ▪ Proficient in testing techniques ▪ Understands various testing phases
▪ Follows test standards	▪ Proficient in GUI design standards

---

2. The term **usability** refers to the intuitiveness and ease-of-use of an application's user interface.

Automated Test Engineer (Automater/Developer)

Responsibilities	Skills
▪ Designs and develops test procedures and cases based upon requirements	▪ Good understanding of GUI design
▪ Designs, develops and executes reusable and maintainable automated scripts ▪ Uses capture/playback tools for GUI automation and/or develops test harnesses using a development or scripting language, as applicable	▪ Proficient in software testing
▪ Follows test-design standards	▪ Proficient in designing test suites
▪ Conducts/Attends test procedure walk-throughs	▪ Proficient in working with test tools
▪ Executes tests and prepares reports on test progress and regression	▪ Programming skills
▪ Attends test-tool user groups and related activities to remain abreast of test-tool capabilities	▪ Proficient in GUI design standards

Network Test Engineer

Responsibilities	Skills
▪ Performs network, database, and middleware testing	▪ Network, database and system administration skills
▪ Researches network, database, and middleware performance monitoring tools ▪ Develops load and stress test designs, cases, and procedures ▪ Supports walk-throughs or inspections of load and stress test procedures	▪ Expertise in a variety of technical skills, including programming languages, database technologies, and computer operating systems
▪ Implements performance monitoring tools on ongoing basis ▪ Conducts load and stress testing	▪ Product evaluation and integration skills ▪ Familiarity with network sniffers, and available tools for load and stress testing

Test Environment Specialist

Responsibilities	Skills
• Responsible for installing test tool and establishing test-tool environment	• Network, database and system administration skills
• Responsible for creating and controlling test environment by using environment setup scripts	• Expertise in a variety of technical skills, including programming and scripting languages, database technologies, and computer operating systems
• Creates and maintains test database (adds/restores/deletes, etc)	• Test tool and database experience
• Maintains requirements hierarchy within test-tool environment	• Product evaluation and integration skills

Security Test Engineer

Responsibilities	Skills
• Responsible for security testing of the application	• Understands security testing techniques • Background in security • Security test tool experience

Test Library and Configuration Specialist [a]

Responsibilities	Skills
• Test-script change management	• Network, database, and system administration skills
• Test-script version control	• Expertise in a variety of technical skills including programming languages, database technologies, and computer operating systems
• Maintaining test-script reuse library • Creating the various test builds, in some cases	• Configuration-management tool expertise
	• Test-tool experience

a. This type of configuration is often done by a separate configuration management department.

It is important that the appropriate roles be assigned to the right people, based on their skill sets and other strengths. Individual testers can specialize in specific areas of the application, as well as nonfunctional areas. Assigning testers to specific areas of the application may enable them to become experts in those specific areas. In addition to focusing on particular functional testing areas, different team members should specialize in specific nonfunctional testing areas, performance testing, compatibility, security, and concurrency.

Teams that use automated test tools should include personnel with software-development skills. Automated testing requires that test scripts be developed, executed, and managed. For this reason, the skills and activities pertinent to performing manual testing differ from those required for performing automated software testing. Because of this difference, manual test roles should be listed separately in the definition of roles and responsibilities. This does not mean that an "automated test engineer" won't be expected to do some manual testing from time to time.

If multiple products are under test, testers can maximize continuity by keeping specific team members assigned to the same product domains for some period of time. It can be difficult for testers to switch between significantly different technical or problem domains too often. Testers should be kept on either the same type of products (e.g., Web vs. desktop applications) or in the same problem areas, depending on where their strengths lie. The most effective testers understand the business and system requirements, in addition to being technically adept.

Table 13.2 gives an example of a test-team structure. Basic skills are assumed and not listed. For example, if working in a Windows environment, it is assumed that the team members have Windows skills; if working in a UNIX environment, it is assumed the team members have basic UNIX skills.

Table 13.2 Example Test-Team Assignments

Position	Products	Duties / Skills	Roles and Responsibilities
Test Manager	Desktop Web	Responsible for test program, customer interface, test-tool introduction, and staff recruiting and supervision Skills: Management skills, MS Project, Winrunner, SQL, SQL Server, UNIX, VC++, Web applications, test-tool experience	Manage test program *(continued)*

Table 13.2 Example Test-Team Assignments (cont.)

Position	Products	Duties / Skills	Roles and Responsibilities
Test Lead	Desktop Web	Staff supervision, cost/progress/test status reporting, and test planning, design, development, and execution Skills: TeamTest, Purify, Visual Basic, SQL, Winrunner, Robot, UNIX, MS Access, C/C++, SQL Server	[Reference the related testing requirements here] Develop automated test scripts for functional test procedures
Test Engineer	Desktop Web	Test planning, design, development, and execution Defect identification and tracking Skills: Test-tool experience, financial system experience	[Reference the related testing requirements here] Develop test harness
Test Engineer	Desktop Web	Test planning, design, development, and execution Defect identification and tracking Skills: Test-tool experience, financial system experience	Performance testing [Reference the related testing requirements here]
Test Engineer	Desktop	Test planning, design, development, and execution Defect identification and tracking Skills: Financial system experience	Configuration testing, installation testing [Reference the related testing requirements here]

(continued)

Table 13.2 Example Test-Team Assignments (cont.)

Position	Products	Duties / Skills	Roles and Responsibilities
Test Engineer	Web	Responsible for test tool environment, network, and middleware testing Performs all other test activities Defect identification and tracking Skills: Visual Basic, SQL, CNE, UNIX, C/C++, SQL Server	Security testing [Reference the related testing requirements here]
Jr. Test Engineer	Desktop	Performs test planning, design, development, and execution Defect identification and tracking Skills: Visual Basic, SQL, UNIX, C/C++, HTML, MS Access	[Reference the related testing requirements here]

Table 13.2 identifies test-team positions and their assignments on the project, together with the products they are working on. The duties that must be performed by the person in each of the positions are outlined, as are the skills of the personnel fulfilling those positions. Also noted are the products to which each position on the team is assigned.

Item 1 of this book emphasized the importance of the testing team's involvement from the beginning of the product's life cycle. If early involvement of testers has become an established practice in an organization, it is possible (and necessary) to define and document the role of the testing team during each phase of the life cycle, including the deliverables expected from the testing team upon completion of each phase.

Item 14: Require a Mixture of Testing Skills, Subject-Matter Expertise, and Experience

The most effective testing team consists of team members with a mixture of expertise, such as subject matter, technology, and testing techniques, plus a mixture of experience levels, such as beginners and expert testers. Subject-matter experts (SMEs) who understand the details of the application's functionality play an important role in the testing team.

The following list describes these concepts in more detail.

- *Subject matter expertise.* A technical tester might think it is feasible to learn the subject matter in depth, but this is usually not the case when the domain is complex. Some problem domains, such as tax law, labor contracts, and physics, may take years to fully understand. It could be argued that detailed and specific requirements should include all the complexities possible, so that the developer can properly design the system and the tester can properly plan the testing. Realistically, however, budget and time constraints often lead to requirements that are insufficiently detailed, leaving the content open to interpretation. Even detailed requirements often contain internal inconsistencies that must be identified and resolved.

    For these reasons, each SME must work closely with the developer and other SMEs on the program (for example, tax-law experts, labor-contracts experts, physicists) to parse out the intricacies of the requirements. Where there are two SMEs, they must be in agreement. If two SMEs cannot agree, a third SME's input is required. A testing SME will put the final stamp of approval on the implementation, after appropriate testing.

- *Technical expertise.* While it is true that a thorough grasp of the domain is a valuable and desirable trait for a tester, the tester's effectiveness will be diminished without some level of understanding of software (including test) engineering. The most effective subject-matter expert testers are those who are also interested and experienced in the technology—that is, those who have taken one or more programming courses, or have some related technical experience. Subject-matter knowledge must be complemented with technical knowledge, including an understanding of the science of software testing.

  Technical testers, however, require a deeper knowledge of the technical platforms and architectural makeup of a system in order to test successfully. A technical tester should know how to write automated scripts; know how to write a test harness; and understand such technical issues as compatibility, performance, and installation, in order to be best prepared to test for compliance. While it is beneficial for SMEs to possess some of this knowledge, it is acceptable, of course, for them to possess a lower level of technical expertise than do technical testers.

- *Experience level.* A testing team is rarely made up exclusively of expert testers with years of expertise—nor would that necessarily be desirable. As with all efforts, there is room for apprentices who can be trained and mentored by more-senior personnel. To identify potential areas for training and advancement, the test manager must review the difference between the skill requirements and an individual's actual skills.

  A junior tester could be tasked with testing the lower-risk functionality, or cosmetic features such as the GUI interface controls (if this area is considered low-risk). If a junior tester is tasked with testing of higher-risk functionality, the junior tester should be paired with a more-senior tester who can serve as a mentor.

Although technical and subject-matter testers contribute to the testing effort in different ways, collaboration between the two types of testers should be encouraged. Just as it would take a technical tester a long time to get up to speed on all the details of the subject matter, it would take a domain or subject-matter expert a long time to become conversant with the technical issues to consider during testing. Cross-training should be provided to make the technical tester acquainted with the subject matter and the subject-matter expert familiar with the technical issues.

Some testing tasks may require specific skills within the technical or subject-matter area. For example, a tester who is experienced, or at least familiar, with usability testing techniques should be responsible for usability testing. A tester who is not skilled in this area can only guess what makes an application usable. Similarly, in the case of localization testing, an English speaker can only guess regarding the correct translation of a Web site into another language. A more effective localization tester would be a native speaker of the language into which the site has been translated.

Item 15: Evaluate the Tester's Effectiveness[1]

Maintaining an effective test program requires that the implementation of its elements, such as test strategy, test environment, and test-team make-up, be continuously evaluated, and improved as needed. Test managers are responsible for ensuring that the testing program is being implemented as planned and that specific tasks are being executed as expected. To accomplish this, they must track, monitor, and evaluate the implementation of the test program, so it can be modified as needed.

At the core of test-program execution are the test engineers. The ability of testers to properly design, document, and execute effective tests, accurately interpret the results, document any defects, and track them to closure is critical to the effectiveness of the testing effort. A test manager may plan the perfect testing process and select the ideal strategy, but if the test-team members do not effectively execute the testing process (for example, participating effectively in requirements inspections and design walk-throughs) and complete all strategic testing tasks as assigned (such as executing specific test procedures), important defects may be discovered too late in the development life cycle, resulting in increased costs. Worse, defects may be completely overlooked, and make their way into production software.

A tester's effectiveness can also make a big difference in relationships with other project groups. A tester who frequently finds bogus errors, or reports "user errors"

---

1. Adapted from Elfriede Dustin, "Evaluating a Tester's Effectiveness," *Stickyminds.com* (Mar. 11, 2002). See http://www.effectivesoftwaretesting.com.

when the application works as expected but the tester misunderstands the requirement, or (worst of all) often overlooks critical defects loses credibility with other team members and groups, and can tarnish the reputation of an entire test program.

Evaluating a tester's effectiveness is a difficult and often subjective task. Besides the typical elements in any employee's performance, such as attendance, attentiveness, attitude, and motivation, there are specific testing-related measures against which a tester can be evaluated. For example, all testers must be detail oriented and possess analytical skills, independent of whether they are technical testers, subject-matter experts, security testers, or usability testers.

The evaluation process starts with recruitment. The first step is to hire a tester with the skills required for the roles and responsibilities assigned to each position. (See Item 13 for a discussion on roles, responsibilities, and skills.)

In the case where a testing team is "inherited" rather than hired for the project, evaluation is more complicated. In such a case it is necessary for the manager to become familiar with the various testers' backgrounds, so the team members can be tasked and evaluated based on their experience, expertise, and backgrounds. It may become necessary to reassign some team members to other roles as their abilities become better known.

A test engineer's performance cannot be evaluated unless there are specified roles and responsibilities, tasks, schedules, and standards. The test manager must, first and foremost, state clearly what is expected of the test engineer, and by when.

Following is a typical list of expectations that must be communicated to testers.

- *Observe standards and procedures.* The test engineer must be aware of standards and procedures to be followed, and processes must be communicated. Standards and procedures are discussed in Item 21.

- *Keep schedules.* Testers must be aware of the test schedule, including when test plans, test designs, test procedures, scripts, and other testing products must be delivered. In addition, the delivery schedule of software components to testing should be known by all testers.

- *Meet goals and perform assigned tasks.* Tasks must be documented and communicated, and deadlines must be scheduled, for each tester. The test manager and the test engineer must agree on the assigned tasks.

- *Meet budgets.* For testers evaluating testing tools or other technology that must be purchased, the available budget must be communicated so the tester can work within that range and avoid wasting time evaluating products that are too expensive.

Expectations and assignments differ depending on the task at hand and the skill set of the tester. Different types of tests, test approaches, techniques, and outcomes may be expected.

Once expectations are set, the test manager can start comparing the work of the test team against the established goals, tasks, and schedules to measure effectiveness of implementation. Following is a list of points to consider when evaluating a tester's effectiveness.

- *Subject-matter expert vs. technical expert.* The expertise expected from a subject-matter expert is related to the domain of the application, while a technical tester is concerned with the technical issues of the application.

  When a technical tester functions as an automater, automated test procedures should be evaluated based on defined standards that must be followed by the test engineers. For example, the supervisor might ask: Did the engineer create maintainable, modular, reusable automated scripts, or do the scripts have to be modified with each new system build? Did the tester follow best practices, such as making sure the test database was baselined and could be restored when the automated scripts need to be rerun? If the tester is developing custom test scripts or a test harness, the tester will be evaluated on some of the same criteria as a developer, including readability and reliability of the code.

  A tester who specializes in the use of automated tools, yet does not understand the intricacies of the application's functionality and underlying concepts, will usually be ineffective. Automated scripts based only on high-level knowledge of the application will often find less-important defects. It is important that the automater understand the application's functionality in order to be an effective member of the testing team.

  Another area for evaluation is technical ability and adaptability. Is the test engineer capable of picking up new tools and becoming familiar with their capabilities? Testers should be trained regarding the various capabilities of a testing tool, if they are not already thoroughly familiar with them.

- *Experienced vs. novice tester.* As previously mentioned, the skill level of the tester must be taken into account. For example, novice testers may overlook some errors, or not realize they are defects. It is important to assign novice testers to lower-risk testing areas.

  Inexperienced testers are not alone in overlooking defects. Experienced testers may ignore some classes of defects based on past experience ("the product has always done that") or the presence of work-arounds. Appropriately or not, testers may become "acclimated" to familiar errors, and may not report defects that seem unimportant to them but may be unacceptable to end users.

- *Functional vs. nonfunctional testing.* A tester's understanding of the various testing techniques available (see Chapter 5) and knowledge of which technique is most effective for the task at hand should be evaluated. If the tester doesn't understand the various techniques and applies a technique inappropriately, test designs, test cases, and test procedures will be adversely affected.

  Functional testing can additionally be based on a review of the test procedures. Typically, testers are assigned to test procedures for testing specific areas of functionality based on assigned requirements. Test procedure walk-throughs and inspections should be conducted that include the requirements, testing, and development teams. During the walk-through, it should be verified that all teams agree on the behavior of the application.

  The following questions should be considered during an evaluation of functional test procedures:

  - How completely are the test-procedure steps mapped to the requirements steps? Is traceability complete?

  - Are the test input, steps, and output (expected result) correct?

  - Are major testing steps omitted in the functional flow of the test procedure?

  - Has an analytical thought process been applied to produce effective test scenarios?

  - Have the test-procedure creation standards been followed?

- How many revisions have been required as a result of misunderstanding or miscommunication before the test procedures could be considered effective and complete?

- Have effective testing techniques been used to derive the appropriate set of test cases?

During a test-procedure walk-through, the "depth" or thoroughness of the test procedure should be verified. In other words, what does the test procedure test? Does it test functionality only at a high level, or does it really dig deep down into the underlying functionality of the application?

To some extent, this is related to the depth of the requirement steps. For example, a functional requirement might state, "The system should allow for adding records of type A." A high-level test procedure establishes that the record can be added through the GUI. A more-effective test procedure also includes steps that test the areas of the application affected when this record is added. For instance, a SQL statement might verify that the record appears correctly in the database tables. Additional steps could verify the record type. There are numerous other testing steps to be considered, such as verifying the system's behavior when adding multiple records of type A—whether duplicates are allowed, for example.

If test procedures are at a very high level, it is important to confirm that the requirements are at the appropriate level and pertinent details are not missing. If there is a detail in the requirement that is missing in the test procedure, the test engineer might need coaching on how to write effective test procedures. Or, it could be that the engineer did not adequately understand the requirement.

Different criteria apply to evaluating functional testing than to nonfunctional testing. For example, nonfunctional tests must be designed and documented in a different manner than functional test procedures.

- *Testing phase.* Different tasks are to be performed by the tester depending on the testing phase (alpha test, beta test, system test, acceptance test, and so on).

During system testing, the tester is responsible for all testing tasks described in this book, including the development and execution of test procedures, tracking defects to closure, and so on. Other testing phases may be less comprehensive.

During alpha testing, for example, a tester might be tasked with simply recreating and documenting defects reported by members of a separate "alpha testing team," which is usually the company's independent testing (Independent Verification and Validation, or IV&V) team.

During beta testing, a tester might be tasked with documenting the beta-test procedures to be executed, in addition to recreating and documenting defects found by other beta testers. (Customers are often recruited to become beta testers.)

- *Phase of the development life cycle.* As mentioned throughout this book, testers should be involved from the beginning of the life cycle. Evaluation of tester performance should be appropriate to each phase. For example, during the requirements phase, the tester can be evaluated based on defect-prevention efforts, such as identification of testability issues or requirements inconsistencies.

  While a tester's evaluation can be subjective, many variables related to the phase of testing must be considered, rather than jumping to the first seemingly obvious conclusion. For example, when evaluating the test engineer during the requirements phase, it is important to consider the quality of the requirements themselves. If the requirements are poorly written, even an average tester can find many defects. However, if the requirements are well laid out and their quality is above average, only an exceptional tester is likely to find the most subtle defects.

- *Following of instructions and attention to detail.* It is important to consider how well a test engineer follows instructions and pays attention to detail. Reliability and follow-through must be monitored. If test procedures must be updated and executed to ensure a quality product, the test manager must be confident that the test engineers will carry out this task. If tests have to be automated, the test manager should be confident that progress is being made.

  Weekly status meetings where engineers report on their progress are useful to track and measure progress. In the final stages of a testing phase, these meetings may be held daily.

- *Types of defects, defect ratio, and defect documentation.* The types of defects found by the engineer must be considered during the evaluation. When using this metric to evaluate a tester's effectiveness, some factors to keep in mind include the skill level of the tester, the types of tests being performed, the testing phase being conducted, and the complexity and the maturity of the application under test. Finding defects depends not only upon the skill of the tester, but also on the skill of the developer who wrote, debugged, and unit tested the code, and on the walk-through and inspection teams that reviewed the requirements, design, and code. Ideally, they will have corrected most defects before formal testing.

An additional factor to evaluate in this context is whether the test engineer finds errors that are complex and domain related, or only cosmetic. Cosmetic defects, such as missing window text or control placement, are relatively easy to detect and become high priority during usability testing, whereas more complicated problems relating to data or cause-effect relationships between elements in the application are more difficult to detect, require a better understanding of the application, and become high priority during functional testing. On the other hand, cosmetic-defect fixes, since they are most visible, may have a more immediate effect on customer happiness.

The test manager must consider the area for which the tester is responsible. The tester responsible for a specific area where the most defects are discovered in production should not necessarily be assumed to have performed poorly. If the tester's area is very complex and error-prone and the product was released in a hurry, failure to catch some defects may be understandable.

The *types* of defects discovered in production also matter. If they could have been discovered by a basic test within the existing test-procedure suite, and if there was plenty of time to execute the test procedure, this would be a major oversight by the tester responsible for this area. However, before passing judgment, some additional questions should be considered:

- Was the test procedure supposed to be executed manually? The manual tester may have become tired of executing the same test procedures over and over, and after many trials concluded it should be safe not to execute the tests because that part of the application has always worked in the past.

- Was the software delivered under pressure of a deadline that could not be changed even though it ruled out a full test cycle? Releases should not be allowed without having met the release criteria, time pressures notwithstanding.

- Was this test automated? Did the automated script miss testing the step containing the error? In such a case, the automated scripts must be reevaluated.

- Was the defect discovered using some combination of functional steps that are rarely executed? This type of defect is more understandable.

Additionally, it may be necessary to review the test goals, risks of the project, and assumptions made when the test effort started. If it had been decided not to conduct a specific type of test because of time constraints or low risk, then the tester should not be held responsible. This risk should have been taken with full knowledge of the possibility of problems.

Effectiveness can also be evaluated by examining how a defect is documented. Is there enough detail in the documented defect for a developer to be able to recreate the problem, or do developers have a difficult time recreating one specific tester's defects? Standards must be in place that document precisely what information is required in defect documentation, and the defect tracking life cycle must be well communicated and understood. All testers must follow these standards. (For a discussion of the defect tracking life cycle, see Item 50.)

For each issue uncovered during evaluation of a tester, the cause of the issue should be determined and a solution should be sought. Each issue must be evaluated with care before a judgment regarding the tester's capability is made. After careful evaluation of the entire situation, and after additional coaching has been provided where called for, it will be possible to evaluate how detail oriented, analytical, and effective this tester is. If it is determined that the tester lacks attention to detail or analytical skills or there are communication issues, that tester's performance may need to be closely monitored and reviewed, and there may be a need for additional instruction and training, or other appropriate steps need to be taken.

Testers' effectiveness must be constantly evaluated to ensure the success of the testing program.

TEST ENGINEER SELF-EVALUATION

Test engineers should assume responsibility for evaluating their own effectiveness. The following list of issues can be used as a starting-point in developing a process for test-engineer self-evaluation, assuming roles and responsibilities along with task assignments are understood:

- Consider the types of defects being discovered. Are they important, or are they mostly cosmetic, low-priority defects? If the tester consistently uncovers only low-priority defects—such as, during functional testing, non-working hot keys, or typographical errors in the GUI—the effectiveness of the test procedures should be reassessed. Keep in mind that during other testing phases (for the examples mentioned here, during usability testing), the priority of certain defects will change.

- Are test procedures detailed enough, covering the depth, and combinations and variations of data and functional paths, necessary to catch the higher-priority defects? Do tests include invalid data as well as valid data?

- Was feedback regarding test procedures received and incorporated from requirements and development staff, and from other testers? If not, the test engineer should ask for test-procedure reviews, inspections, and walk-throughs involving those teams.

- Does the test engineer understand the range of testing techniques available, such as boundary-values testing, equivalence partitioning, and orthogonal arrays, well enough to select the most effective test procedures?

- Does the engineer understand the intricacies of the application's functionality and domain well? If not, the tester should ask for an overview or additional training. A technical tester may ask for help from a Subject-Matter Expert (SME).

- Are major defects being discovered too late in the testing cycle? If this occurs regularly, the following points should be considered:

  Does the initial testing focus on low-priority requirements? Initial testing should focus on the high-priority, highest-risk requirements.

  Does the initial testing focus on regression testing of existing functionality that was working previously and rarely broke in the past? Initial testing should focus on code changes, defect fixes, and new functionality. Regression testing should come later. Ideally, the regression-testing efforts can be automated, so test engineers can focus on the newer areas.

- Are any areas under testing exhibiting suspiciously low defect counts? If so, these areas should be re-evaluated to determine:

  Whether the test coverage is sufficiently robust.

Whether the types of tests being performed are most effective. Are important steps missing?

Whether the application area under test has low complexity, so that indeed it may be error-free.

Whether the functionality was implemented in such a manner that it is likely no major defects remain—for example, if it was coded by the most senior developers and has already been unit and integration tested well.

Consider the Defect Workflow:

- Each defect should be documented in a timely manner (i.e., as soon as it is discovered and verified)

- Defect-documentation standards must be followed. If there aren't any defect-documentation standards, they should be requested from the engineer's manager. The standards should list all information that must be included in documenting a defect to enable the developer to reproduce it.

- If a new build is received, initial testing should focus on retesting the defects. It is important that supposedly fixed defects be retested as soon as possible, so the developers know whether their repair efforts are successful.

- Comments received from the development team regarding the quality of defect reports should be continually evaluated. If the reports are often said to lack required information, such as a full description of testing steps required to reproduce the errors, the testers should work on providing better defect documentation.

- Testers should be eager to track defects to closure.

- Examine the comments added to defect documentation to determine how developers or other testers receive it. If defects are often marked "works as expected" or "cannot be reproduced," it could also signal some problems:

  - The tester's understanding of the application may be inadequate. In this case, more training is required. Help may be requested from domain SMEs.

  - The requirements may be ambiguous. If so, they must be clarified. (Most commonly, this is discovered during the requirements or test-procedure walk-through and inspections.)

- The engineer's documentation skills may not be as effective as necessary. Inadequate documentation may lead to misunderstanding of the identified defect. The description may need additional steps to enable developers to reproduce the error.

- The developer may be misinterpreting the requirement.

- The developer may lack the patience to follow the detailed documented defect steps to reproduce the defect.

- The tester should monitor whether defects are being discovered in that person's test area after the application has gone to production. Any such defects should be evaluated to determined why they were missed:

  - Did the tester fail to execute a specific test procedure that would have caught this defect? If so, why was the procedure overlooked? Are regression tests automated?

  - Was there no test procedure that would have caught this defect? If so, why not? Was this area considered low risk? The test procedure creation strategy should be reevaluated, and a test procedure should be added to the regression test suite to catch errors like the one in question. The tester should discuss with peers or a manager how to create more effective test procedures, including test design, strategy, and technique.

  - Was there not enough time to execute an existing test procedure? If so, management should be informed—before the application goes live or is shipped, not after the fact. This sort of situation should also be discussed in a post-test/pre-installation meeting, and should be documented in the test report.

- Do other testers during the course of their work discover defects that were this tester's responsibility? If so, the tester should evaluate the reasons and make adjustments accordingly.

There are many more questions a tester can ask related to testing effectiveness, depending on the testing phase and testing task at hand, type of expertise (technical vs. domain), and tester's experience level.

An automater might want to be sure to become familiar with automation standards and best automation practices. A performance tester might request additional training in the performance-testing tool used and performance testing techniques available.

Self-assessment of the tester's capabilities and the improvement steps that follow are important parts of an effective testing program.

CHAPTER 4

The System Architecture

Proper testing of an application requires more than simply verifying the simulated or re-created user actions. Testing the system through the user interface only, without understanding the system's internal structure and components, is typically referred to as **black-box testing**. By itself, black-box testing is not the most effective way to test. In order to design and implement the most effective strategy for thoroughly investigating the correct functioning of an application, the testing team must have a certain degree of knowledge of the system's internals, such as its major architectural components. Such knowledge enables the testing team to design better tests and perform more effective defect diagnosis. Testing a system or application by directly targeting the various modules and layers of the system is referred to as **gray-box** testing.

Understanding the components and modules that make up an entire system enables the testing team to narrow down its effort and focus on the specific area or layer where a defect is present, increasing the efficiency of the defect-correction activities of the development staff. A black-box tester is limited to reporting on the effect or symptom of a defect, since this tester must rely on the error messages or other information displayed by the interface, such as "the report cannot be generated." A black-box tester also has a more difficult time identifying false positives and false negatives. A gray-box tester, on the other hand, not only sees the error message through the user interface but also has the tools to diagnose the problem and can report on the source of the defect. Understanding the system architecture also allows focused testing to be performed, targeted at architecturally sensitive areas of the application such as the database server or core calculation modules.

Just as it is important for the testing team to be involved during the requirement-writing process, as discussed in Chapter 1, so too must the testing team review the architecture of the application. This allows the team to identify potential testability issues early in the project's life cycle. For example, if an application's architecture makes heavy use of third-party products, this may make the system difficult to test and diagnose, since the organization does not control the source code for these components and cannot modify them. The testing team must identify these types of issues early on to allow for development of an effective testing strategy that takes them into consideration. Overly complex architectures, such as those that make use of many loosely connected off-the-shelf products, can also result in systems whose defects cannot readily be isolated or reproduced. Again, the testing team needs to detect these issues early, to allow for better planning.

The system itself, if implemented correctly, can make for an easier testing process in many ways. Logging or **tracing** mechanisms can be extremely useful in tracking application behavior during development and testing. In addition, different operating **modes**, such as debug and release modes, can be useful in detecting and diagnosing problems with the application even after it has gone live.

Item 16: Understand the Architecture and Underlying Components

An understanding of the architecture and underlying components of an application allows the test engineer to help pinpoint the various areas of the application that produce particular test outcomes. Such an understanding allows the tester to conduct gray-box testing, which can complement the black-box testing approach. During gray-box testing, the tester can identify specific parts of the application that are failing. For example, the test engineer is able to probe areas of the system that are more prone to failure because of their complexity, or simply due to the instability of "fresh" code.

Following are some examples of how a thorough understanding of the system architecture can assist a test engineer:

- *Enhanced defect reporting.* For the most part, test procedures are based on requirements, and therefore have a somewhat fixed path through the system. When an error occurs along this path, the ability of the tester to include information relevant to the system architecture in the defect report can be of great benefit to the system's development staff. For example, if a certain dialog box fails to display, the tester's investigation could determine that it was due to a problem retrieving information from the database, or that the application failed to make a connection to a server.

- *Improved ability to perform exploratory testing.* Once a test has failed, the tester usually must perform some focused testing, perhaps by modifying the original test scenario to determine the application's "breaking point," the factors that cause the system to break. During this exercise, architectural knowledge of the system under test can be of great help to the tester, enabling the test engineer to perform more useful and specific testing—or perhaps to skip additional testing altogether, when knowledge of the underlying components provides adequate information about the problem. For example, if it is known that the application has encountered a connection problem with the database, it is not necessary to attempt the operation with different data values. Instead, the tester can focus on the connection issues.

- *Increased testing precision.* Gray-box testing is designed to exercise the application, either though the user interface or directly against the underlying components, while monitoring internal component behavior to determine the success or failure of the test. Gray-box testing thus naturally produces information relevant to the cause of the defect.

  Here are the most common types of problems that can be encountered during testing:

  - A component encounters a failure of some kind, causing the operation to be aborted. The user interface typically indicates that an error has occurred.

  - The test execution produces incorrect results, different from the expected outcome. Somewhere in the system, a component has processed data incorrectly, causing the erroneous results.

  - A component fails during execution, but does not notify the user interface that an error has occurred, which is known as a false positive. For example, data is entered but is not stored in the database, yet no error is reported to the user.

  - The system reports an error, but it actually has processed everything correctly—the test produces a false negative.

In the first case—an error leads to aborting the operation—it is important to display useful and descriptive error messages, but this often does not occur. For example, if a database error occurs during an operation, the typical user interface displays a cryptic message like "failed to complete operation," without any details as to why. A much more useful error message would give more information, such as, "failed to complete operation due to a database error."

Internally, the application may also have an error log with even more information. Knowledge of the system components allows the tester to use all available
tools, including log files and other monitoring mechanisms, to more precisely
test the system, rather than depending entirely on user-interface messages.

There are several ways that the testing team can gain an understanding of the
architecture. Perhaps the best way is for the team to participate in architecture and
design reviews where the development staff presents the proposed architecture. In
addition, testers should be encouraged to review architecture and design documentation and to ask questions of the developers. It is also important that the testing
team review any changes to the architecture after each release, so that any impact on
the testing effort can be assessed.

Item 17: Verify That the System Supports Testability

Most large systems are made up of many subsystems, which in turn consist of code residing in one or more layers and other supporting components, such as databases and message queues. Users interact with the boundaries, or user interface, of the system, which then interacts with other subsystems to complete a task. The more subsystems, layers, and components there are in a system, the more difficult it may be to isolate a problem while testing that system.

Consider the following example. The user interface takes input from the user, and, using the services of various layers of code in the application, eventually writes that input to a database. Later, another subsystem, such as a reporting system, reads the data and performs some additional processing to produce a report. If something goes wrong in any part of this process, perhaps due to a problem with the user's data or a concurrency problem, the location of the defect can be difficult to isolate, and the error may be difficult to recreate.

When the architecture of an application is first being conceptualized, the testers should have an opportunity to ask questions about how they can follow input through a path within the system. For example, if a certain function causes a task to be launched on another server, it is useful for the tester to have a way to verify that the remote task was indeed launched as required. If the proposed architecture makes it difficult to track this kind of interaction, then it may be necessary to reconsider the approach, perhaps using a more dependable, and testable, architecture. The testing strategy must account for these types of issues, and may require an integrated test effort in some cases with staff from other development efforts, including third-party component vendors.

The testing team must consider all aspects of the proposed architecture, and how they may or may not contribute to effective and efficient testing of the application. For example, although third-party components, such as off-the-shelf user-interface controls, can reduce development time by obviating large sections of work on architecturally significant components, their use may have negative implications for testability. Unless the source code is available—and can be modified—it may be difficult to follow paths through third-party components, which may not provide tracing or other diagnostic information. If using a third-party component is proposed for the application's architecture, it is important to prototype the implementation and verify that there are ways to monitor the flow of control through that component. Third-party components may also prevent the use of some testing tools, which in turn can adversely affect the testing effort.

Investigating the testability of an application's architecture while it exists only on paper can greatly reduce the number of testing surprises that may be encountered later on. If the testing implications of one or more aspects of the architecture are unclear, the test team should insist on a prototype that allows the testers to experiment with various testing techniques. Feedback from this exercise can ensure that the application is developed in such a way that its quality can be verified.

Item 18: Use Logging to Increase System Testability

One of the most common ways to increase the testability of an application is to implement a logging, or tracing, mechanism that provides information about what components are doing, including the data upon which they are operating, and about application states or errors encountered while the application is running. Test engineers can use such information to track the processing flow during the execution of a test procedure and to determine where errors are occurring in the system.

As the application executes, all components write log entries detailing what **methods** (also known as **functions**) they are currently executing and the major objects they are manipulating. Entries are typically written to a disk file or database, properly formatted for analysis or debugging at some point in the future, after the execution of one or more test procedures. In a complex client-server or Web system, log files may be written on several machines, so it is important that the logs include enough information to determine the path of execution between machines.

The tracing mechanism must write enough information to the log to be useful for analysis and debugging, but not so much information that it creates an overwhelming and unhelpful volume of information, making it difficult to isolate important entries.

A log **entry** is simply a formatted message that contains key information that can be used during analysis. A well-formed log entry includes the following pieces of information:

- *Class name and method name.* This can be a function name if the function is not a member of any class. This information is important for determining a path of execution through several components.

99

- *Host name and process ID.* This will allow log entries to be compared and tracked if they are generated from events on different machines or from different processes on the same machine.

- *Time-stamp of the entry (to the millisecond or better).* An accurate time-stamp on all entries allows the events to be correlated, if they occur in parallel or on different machines, which may cause them to be entered in the log out of sequence.

- *Messages.* One of the most important pieces of the entry is the message. It is a description, written by the developer, of what was happening at the time in the application. A message can also be a description of an error encountered during execution, or a result code from an operation. Other types of messages include the logging of persistent entity IDs or keys of major domain objects. This allows tracking of objects through the system during execution of a test procedure.

By reviewing the items written to the log file by every method or function of every component in the system, the execution of a test procedure can be traced through the system and correlated with the data in the database (if applicable) on which it is operating. In the case of a serious failure, the log records indicate the responsible component. In the case of a computational error, the log file lists all of the components that participated in the execution of the test procedure, and the IDs or keys of all entities used. Along with the entity data from the database, this should be enough information to allow development personnel to isolate the error in the source code.

Following is an example of log records from an application that has retrieved a customer object from a database:

```
Function:  main (main.cpp, line 100)
Machine:   testsrvr (PID=2201)
Timestamp: 1/10/2002 20:26:54.721
Message:   connecting to database [dbserver1, customer_db]

Function:  main (main.cpp, line 125)
Machine:   testsrvr (PID=2201)
Timestamp: 1/10/2002 20:26:56.153
Message:   successfully connected to database
           [dbserver1, customer_db]

Function:  retrieveCustomer (customer.cpp line 20)
Machine:   testsrvr (PID=2201)
Timestamp: 1/10/2002 20:26:56.568
Message:   attempting to retrieve customer record
           for customer ID [A1000723]
```

```
Function:  retrieveCustomer (customer.cpp line 25)
Machine:   testsrvr (PID=2201)
Timestamp: 1/10/2002 20:26:57.12
Message:   ERROR: failed to retrieve customer record,
           message [customer record for ID A1000723
           not found]
```

This log-file excerpt demonstrates a few of the major aspects of application logging that can be used for effective testing.

In each entry, the function name is indicated, along with the file name and the line number of the application source code that generated the entry. The host and process ID are also recorded, as well as the time when the entry was made. Each message contains useful information about the identities of components involved in the activity. For example, the database server is "dbserver1," the database is "customer_db," and the customer ID is "A1000723."

From this log, it is evident that the application was not able to successfully retrieve the specified customer record. In this situation, a tester could examine the database on dbserver1 and, using SQL tools, query the customer_db database for the customer record with ID A1000723 to verify its absence.

This information adds a substantial amount of defect-diagnosis capability to the testing effort, since the tester can now pass such detailed information along to the development staff as part of the defect report. The tester can report not only a "symptom" but also internal application behavior that pinpoints the cause of the problem.

Item 19: Verify That the System Supports Debug and Release Execution Modes

W hile a software system is under construction, there obviously will be many malfunctions. Problems may surface anytime during developer testing, particularly in the unit and integration test phases and during formal tests by the testing team.

When defects are discovered, there must be a way to diagnose the problem, preferably without any modifications to the application itself. To make this process efficient, the application must support different operating modes, particularly a **debug mode** to help developers and testers diagnose problems as they are encountered, and a **release mode**, an optimized version of the system stripped of most or all of its debugging-related features. The application is usually delivered to end users in release mode.

Depending on the languages, tools, and platforms involved in an application's development, there are several ways it can be debugged.

- *Source-code inspection.* If a problem is not terribly complex, a visual inspection of the source code may be enough to determine the problem. For instance, if an incorrect title bar appears on an application window, the developer can simply look in the source code for the definition of the window's title bar text and change it accordingly.

- *Logging output.* If the application has a logging mechanism, as described in Item 18, the developer can run the application, re-create the error, and then

103

examine the log entries that were generated. Better still, the tester will have provided a log-file excerpt in the defect report. If the excerpt contains enough information for the developer to determine the cause of the problem, the defect can then be corrected in the source code. Otherwise, the developer may have to consider one of the other debugging techniques listed here.

- *Real-time debugging.* In this most powerful debugging technique, the developer "attaches" a debugger to a running instance of the application, and monitors variables and program flow in the debugging environment while interacting directly with the application. Defects are re-created by executing the steps in a defect report, the application code is examined while it is running to determine the source of the defect.

Which of these techniques to use is up to the developer, but the information in the defect report usually makes one approach obvious. For example, if the problem is a simple cosmetic issue, a quick examination of the source code is usually all that is necessary. Deeper, more complex issues typically require real-time debugging.

Real-time debugging is not always possible, however. In C++, for example, real-time debugging requires a **debug build** of the system. (Debug code also performs many supplemental checks, such as checks for stack and heap corruption—common when the system is under development.) As mentioned previously, the development environment can be "attached" to the debug build of the application while it is running, allowing the developer to monitor the code while interacting with the application. The application's behavior and variables may thus be thoroughly examined—sometimes the only way to properly diagnose and correct a defect.

In addition, a debug build of an application issues more-verbose messages about problems encountered with respect to memory and other lower-level system functions. For example, when low-level errors or unexpected conditions (**assertions**) are encountered while the application is running, it typically will display a dialog box describing the problem as it occurs. Such low-level, diagnostic messages are not meant for end users and usually will not be displayed by a release build of the system; instead, if there is a problem, the system may simply crash or exhibit unpredictable behavior.

Once the system is ready to ship, it is necessary to disable or remove debugging features. In some languages, this involves rebuilding the system. This is necessary because debugging features, such as logging, usually result in slower performance and higher memory usage, and could exhaust system resources, such as disk space, if left unattended. In addition, excess logging can pose a security risk by possibly exposing information to system intruders.

Since it is possible that an application may exhibit new defects when built in release mode, it is important for the test team to be aware of which build **mode** it is testing. For the most part, only the development staff should work with debug builds; the test team should work with release builds. This will ensure that the release build of the software—the version of the system that will be delivered to customers—receives appropriate attention.

The presence of logging mechanisms must also be considered for a release build of the system. The logging mechanism can be removed from the application altogether, or, preferably, configured to do less logging or none at all. Although it may seem that all logging should be removed from the release version of an application, there can be considerable value in leaving some form of logging enabled. When a configurable logging mechanism is in place in the production version of an application, defects can still effectively be diagnosed even after the application has gone live. Defects discovered by customers can be re-created and diagnosed with the assistance of log files, a more reliable approach than simply attempting to re-create a problem by relying on the user's input and the error messages produced at the application's user interface.

An application's logging mechanism can be made configurable through the use of a configuration file, which specifies the level at which logging should take place. A simple logging system would have two levels, **errors** and **debug information**. In the application's code, a level would be associated with each log entry, and the configuration file would specify the level of logging. Typically, only errors are logged in release mode, whereas both errors and debug statements are logged in debug mode. The following pseudocode illustrates log entries made at each of these two logging levels (errors and debug):

```
write_debug_log_entry "connecting to database"
result = connect_to_database_server "dbserver"
if result == connection_failed then
      write_error_log_entry "failed to connect to database"
else
      write_debug_log_entry "connected to database"
```

The preceding pseudocode demonstrates the logging of both debug and error messages. Debug messages are written to show application flow and data, while error messages are written when problems are encountered (in this example, failure to connect to the database).

When the application is in debug mode, all messages displaying flow, data, and errors are included in the log file. In release mode, only errors are logged. It follows that, in release mode, the log file should not grow too large, since no debug messages are written and errors should not occur frequently after the application has been through several testing cycles.

To ensure that no defects are introduced into the application by the logging mechanism, a regression test must be run to verify that the system behaves the same with the logging mechanism turned on fully (logging both errors and debug messages) or in a reduced capacity (logging errors only, or no logging) before moving the application into production.

Even if logging is removed from the release build of the application, there should be other diagnostic capabilities, since problems can still occur. Diagnosis without logging can be accomplished through the use of system-provided mechanisms, such as the Windows Event Log or UNIX syslog service.

Separate debug and release modes will allow an application to be diagnosed and debugged at different levels of detail depending on the situation. While the application is under development, it is preferable to have full diagnostic logging and debugging capabilities to assist in the isolation and correction of defects. When the application is in production, less diagnostic information is necessary, but some is still desirable in case end users encounter errors. Debug and release builds, as well as configurable logging mechanisms, make this kind of flexibility possible.

CHAPTER 5
Test Design and Documentation

Test design and documentation are among the major functions of a testing team. As discussed in Chapter 1, these activities begin not when a software build is placed into the hands of the testing team, but as soon as the first requirements have been approved and baselined. As requirements and system design are refined over time and through system-development iterations, so are the test procedures refined to cover the new or modified requirements and system functions.

Test procedures can benefit from a structured approach that defines the level at which test procedures will operate—black-box or gray-box; the format for test-procedure documentation; and the testing techniques selected, such as examination of boundary conditions and exploratory testing. In addition, test scripts and other testing software development can benefit from a structured approach that decouples logic from data and implements accepted software design principles.

In evaluating the requirements and the software design, by understanding the architecture, and by reviewing prototypes or an existing application, the testing team can "divide and conquer" the various testing tasks, keeping budgets and schedules in mind. The "what," "how," "when," and "who" of feature testing can be decided by determining a strategy, breaking down the tasks, using a specific technique, and prioritizing the test procedures in a parallel and iterative fashion.

Item 20: Divide and Conquer

With the requirements specifications in hand and some design knowledge to work with, the tester is ready to design and develop the test procedures. When a project has a huge number of requirements, deciding where to start with developing test procedures can seem overwhelming. This Item provides an approach to help break down the testing tasks.

Before test design begins, it is necessary to consider the testing phase in which the tests will be executed. There will be different types of tests appropriate for testing usability, performance, security, and other phases of testing, functional and nonfunctional. Nonfunctional testing is addressed in Chapter 9.

The first step in designing test procedures is to review the test plan, if not already familiar with it, in order to understand the context and framework within which the test objectives, scope, and approach for this testing project are defined. The test plan also lists available resources, such as test equipment and tools; the testing methodology and standards to be followed; and the testing schedule. If a usable test plan (as discussed in Chapter 2) does not already exist, this information must be gathered from other sources.

To break down the testing tasks, the following "what," "when," "how," and "who" questions should be answered.

- *What should be tested?* During the test-planning phase, what to test and what not to test will have been determined and documented as part of the scope of testing.

- *When should test procedures be developed?* In Item 3 we suggest that test procedures be developed as soon as requirements are available. Once it has been determined *what* to test, the sequence of tests must be established. What needs to be tested first? The test planner should get to know the testing priorities, and should become familiar with the build and release schedule. Procedures for testing the high-priority items should be developed first. One exception: Certain functions may need to be run first to "prepare" the system for other functions. These **precursor functions** must be run early, whether they are high priority or not. (For more on prioritizing features, see Item 8.)

Additionally, risk analysis (see Item 7) should be employed to help prioritize test procedures. If it is not possible to test everything, testers are forced to focus on the most critical elements. Risk analysis provides a mechanism for determining which these are.

- **How** *should test procedures be designed?* No single testing solution can effectively cover all parts of a system. Test procedures for the different parts of the system must be designed in the manner most appropriate for effectively testing each of those specific parts.

  In order to design the appropriate and most effective tests, it is necessary to consider the parts that make up the system and how they are integrated. For example, to verify functional behavior of the system via the user interface, test procedures will most likely be based on existing functional-requirements statements, with test cases that execute the various paths and scenarios. Another approach would be to begin by testing each field in the user interface with representative valid and invalid data, verifying the correct behavior for each input. This would involve following a sequence of execution paths, as, for example, when filling one field or screen produces another GUI screen that also requires data input.

  Tests must be designed for GUI testing or back-end testing, or both, depending on the testing strategy previously determined. GUI tests naturally differ from back-end tests.

- **Who** *should develop the tests?* Once it has been determined what must be tested, when it is to be tested, and how the test is to be accomplished, it will be easier to decide to whom the various testing tasks should be assigned, based on the specific roles and responsibilities of the various testers. For a discussion of tester roles and responsibilities see Item 13.

The following additional questions and issues may also arise during the course of test-procedure design and development.

- *What if requirements have not been written?* Without requirements from which to derive test cases, it may be necessary to interview customer representatives, technical staff, and review any available documentation, such as user manuals for the current system (if available yet) or for a legacy system, in order to better understand the application being built. (See Item 5 for a discussion of dangers of basing testing on a legacy product.) If there is a legacy system, design documentation may be available from that system's development process. However, keep in mind that design documents don't necessarily state user requirements correctly. In some cases, it may be necessary to employ reverse engineering of the requirements, and possibly exploratory testing (discussed in Item 27).

- *Black-box and gray-box testing.* Testing that exercises most parts of the system by invoking various system calls through the user interface is called **black-box** testing. For example, if the user adds a record to the application's database by entering data via the user interface, various layers—such as the database layer, the user-interface layer, and business-logic layers—are executed. The black-box tester validates the correct behavior only by viewing the output of the user interface. (See Chapter 4 for more about black-box and gray-box testing.)

   Be aware, however, that in some cases errors may not be reported via the user interface due to defects in the error-reporting mechanism of the software. For example, if the application fails to insert a record in the database but does not report an error to the user interface, the user interface receives a "false positive" from the underlying code and continues on without displaying an error message to the user.

   Since user-interface, or black-box, testing does not exhibit all defects, gray-box testing must also be applied.[1] Gray-box testing, addressed in Item 16, requires test designers to possess knowledge of the underlying components that make up the system.

- *Will a test harness have to be developed?* Some components of a system can be tested only by a test harness. For example, consider a calculation engine that

---

1. Keep in mind that black-box and gray-box testing combined are still not sufficient to produce a quality product. Testing processes, procedures, inspections, and walk-throughs, along with unit and integration testing, are all important parts of effective testing. Black-box and gray-box testing alone cannot identify all of the defects in a software program.

allows for thousands of input combinations. Testing requires a test design different from user-interface or black-box testing: The numbers of combinations and variations of inputs are too huge to test through the user interface. Time and other considerations may require development of a test harness to directly test the calculation engine by entering a large set of input values and verifying the outputs that result. See Item 37 for further discussion.

- *What types of testing techniques should be used?* Various functional-testing techniques are available for deriving the test data and input values required. One technique for verifying large numbers of data combinations is **orthogonal array** testing. Orthogonal array testing allows the selection of the combinations of test parameters that provide maximum coverage using a minimum number of test cases.[2]

  Other testing techniques that can help narrow down a large set of possible input combinations possible are equivalence class partitioning and boundary value analysis (see Item 25). Combining these techniques can result in a narrowed-down, but statistically valuable, set of test inputs.

  Another instance when different types of tests are required is when a **commercial off-the-shelf** (COTS) tool is employed. The proper integration of the COTS tool with the custom code itself must be verified. If, for example, a COTS tool has been certified to execute SQL queries proficiently, tests must still be run to verify that the content of the modified SQL queries is correct.

- *Should a capture/playback tool or other testing tool be used?* While a test harness might be strategically applied for testing the calculation engine or other back-end functions, an automated testing (capture/playback) tool might prove useful for GUI regression testing.

  Defining a testing strategy requires determining which areas of the application should be tested using an automated capture/playback tool, which require a test harness, and which must be tested manually. Testing exclusively with the capture/playback feature of an automated testing tool should be avoided, for reasons discussed in Item 36.

---

2. For more information on orthogonal arrays, see Elfriede Dustin, "Orthogonally Speaking," *STQE Magazine* 3:5 (Sept.-Oct. 2001). Also available at http://www.effectivesoftwaretesting.com.

- *Which tests should be automated?* The test engineer should perform a careful analysis of the application when deciding which tests warrant automation and which should be executed manually. This can help to avoid incurring unnecessary costs, as some tests can be more expensive to automate than to execute manually.

  Here are some examples of tests that could be automated:

  - *Tests that are executed more than once.* By contrast, a test that is executed only once is often not worth automating.

  - *Tests that evaluate high-risk conditions.* Low-risk factors may not be worth testing by automated means. Consider a functional test where there is a miniscule likelihood a user will execute the specific scenario to be tested. For example, the system under test may allow the user to perform actions that, from a business point of view, would not make much sense. The risk associated with scenarios of this type is low, since the number of users affected by its potential failure is low. It doesn't make sense for an automater to concentrate on such issues when designing tests; instead, the focus should be on higher-risk items.

  - *Tests that are run on a regular basis.* Examples include **smoke** (build-verification) tests, regression tests, and mundane tests (tests that include many simple and repetitive steps and must be conducted repeatedly).

  - *Tests that would be impossible, or prohibitively expensive, to perform manually.* For example, automation may be called for when verifying the output of a calculation engine simulating 1,000 multiple-user accesses, during stress and performance testing, during memory-leak detection, or during path-coverage testing.

  - *Tests that have multiple data values for the same actions* (data-driven tests).

  - *Baseline tests to be run on different configurations.*

  - *Tests with predictable results.* It is not cost-effective to automate tests whose outcomes are unpredictable.

  - *Tests on a system that is somewhat stable*, with functionality, implementation, and technology that are not constantly changing. Otherwise, maintenance will outweigh the benefits of automation.

- *What kind of test data is needed?* Once the testing tasks are understood in detail, a set of test data can be defined that provides input to the tests. It is important that test data is chosen carefully—incorrect or oversimplified test data can result in missed or erroneously identified defects, requiring unnecessary work and reducing test coverage. (For more about acquiring test data, see Item 10.)

Answering the questions listed in this Item will help the test planner break down the testing tasks. It is important to consider the available budgets and schedules.

Item 21: Mandate the Use of a Test-Procedure Template and Other Test-Design Standards[1]

For repeatability, consistency, and completeness, the use of a test-procedure template should be mandated when applicable. The following is an example test-procedure template:

TEST PROCEDURE ID:
Follow naming convention—TP ID is based on requirement use cases, but starts with T- instead of R-

TEST NAME:
High-level description of what is being tested

DATE EXECUTED:

TEST ENGINEER INITIALS:

TEST PROCEDURE AUTHOR:

TEST OBJECTIVE
— Briefly describe the purpose of the procedure:

RELATED USE CASE(S)/REQUIREMENT NUMBER(S)
— List any use-case name(s) and number(s) being tested under this test objective:

PRECONDITIONS/ASSUMPTIONS/DEPENDENCIES
— List any conditions, assumptions, and dependencies to be satisfied before these test-procedure steps can be executed. This may be done in a bulleted-list format. Often the same preconditions as in the use case apply here:

---

1. Adapted from Elfriede Dustin et al., "Web Engineering Using the RSI Approach," in *Quality Web Systems: Performance, Security, and Usability* (Boston, Mass.: Addison-Wesley, 2002), 52.

VERIFICATION METHOD:

Functional Testing Steps				Automated / Manual (underline selection)			
Step	User Action (Inputs)	Expected Results	Trace Log Information	Actual Results	Test Data Required	Pass / Fail	Use Case Step # or Requirement Number

Security Testing Steps				Automated / Manual (underline selection)			
Step	User Action (Inputs)	Expected Results	Trace Log Information	Actual Results	Test Data Required	Pass / Fail	Use Case Step # or Requirement Number

Performance Testing Steps				Automated / Manual (underline selection)			
Step	User Action (Inputs)	Expected Results	Trace Log Information	Actual Results	Test Data Required	Pass / Fail	Use Case Step # or Requirement Number

Compatibility Testing Steps				Automated / Manual (underline selection)			
Step	User Action (Inputs)	Expected Results	Trace Log Information	Actual Results	Test Data Required	Pass / Fail	Use Case Step # or Requirement Number

Usability Testing Steps				Automated / Manual (underline selection)			
Step	User Action (Inputs)	Expected Results	Trace Log Information	Actual Results	Test Data Required	Pass / Fail	Use Case Step # or Requirement Number

Figure 21.1—Test Procedure Template

The primary elements of the standard test procedure, shown in Figure 21.1, are:

- *Test Procedure ID:* Use a naming convention for test-procedure IDs.

- *Test Name:* Provide a description of the test procedure.

- *Date Executed:* State when the test procedure was executed.

- *Test Engineer Initials:* Provide the initials of the engineer executing the test procedure.

- *Test Procedure Author:* Identify the developer of the test procedure.

- *Test Objective:* Outline the objective of the test procedure.

- *Related Use Case(s)/Requirement Number(s):* Provide the identification number of the requirement validated by the test procedure.

- *Preconditions/Assumptions/Dependencies:* Provide the criteria, or prerequisites, to be met before the test procedure can be run, such as specific data setup requirements. This field is completed when the test procedure is dependent on a previous test procedure. This field is also completed when two test procedures would conflict if performed at the same time. Note that the precondition for a use case often becomes the precondition for a test procedure.

- *Verification Method:* This field may include certification, automated or manual test, inspection, demonstration, or analysis.

- *User Action (Inputs):* Here, the goals and expectations of a test procedure are clearly defined. This can be accomplished by documenting the steps needed to create a test. The entry in this field may be similar to software-development pseudocode. Completing this field allows for clarification and documentation of the test steps required to verify the use case.

- *Expected Results:* Define the results expected when executing the particular test procedure.

- *Trace Log Information:* Document the behavior of back-end components. During execution, Web system components, for example, write log entries detailing the functions they are executing and the major objects with which they are interacting. These log entries can be captured within the test procedure.

- *Actual Results:* This field may have a default value, such as "Same as Expected Result," that is changed to describe the actual result if the test-procedure fails.

- *Test Data Required:* Reference the set of test data required to support execution of the test procedure. See Item 26 for more detail.

Nonfunctional test considerations are often an afterthought in many testing efforts. However, it is important that nonfunctional tests be considered from the beginning of the testing life cycle. Note that the test-procedure documentation form depicted in Figure 21.1 is divided into five sections—one for functional testing steps and the remainder for the nonfunctional areas of security, performance and scalability, compatibility, and usability. See Item 41 for more information on nonfunctional test considerations.

Test-design standards must be documented, communicated, and enforced so that everyone involved conforms to the design guidelines and produces the required information.[2] Test-procedure creation standards or guidelines are necessary whether developing manual or automated test procedures. The standards for manual test procedures should include an example of how much detail a test procedure should contain. The level of detail may be as simple as outlining the steps to be taken—for example:

Step 1. Click on the File menu.

Step 2. Select Open.

Step 3. Select a directory on the computer's local disk.

Depending on the size of the application being tested, and given the limited schedules and budgets, writing extensive test procedures may be too time-consuming, in which case the high-level test descriptions may be sufficient.

Test-procedure standards can include guidelines on how the expected result of the test is supposed to be documented. The standards should address several questions: Will test results require screen prints? Will tests require sign-off by a second person who observes the execution and result of the test?

When it comes to automated test design standards, standards should be based on best coding practices such as modularity, loose coupling, concise variable and

---

2. Elfriede Dustin et al., *Automated Software Testing* (Reading, Mass.: Addison-Wesley, 1999), Section 7.3.4.

function naming conventions, and so on. These practices are typically the same as those for general software development.

In some situations, not all test scenarios may be documented in the same detail, as a template would require. Some test procedures in complex applications such as financial systems, whose possible inputs to calculations can number in the tens of thousands, may require a different approach to documentation, such as using a spreadsheet.

Item 22: Derive Effective Test Cases from Requirements[1]

A functional test exercises an application with the intent to uncover non-conformance with end-user requirements. This type of testing activity is central to most software test efforts. The primary objective in the functional-testing phase is to assess whether the application does what it is supposed to do in accordance with specified requirements.

A good practice for developing test procedures for the functional testing phase is to base them on the functional requirements. Additionally, some of the test procedures created for this testing phase can be modified for use in testing the nonfunctional aspects of the application, such as performance, security, and usability.

In Chapter 1, the importance of having testable, complete, and detailed requirements was discussed. In practice, however, having a perfect set of requirements at the tester's disposal is a rarity. In order to create effective functional test procedures, the tester must understand the details and intricacies of the application. When, as is often the case, these details and intricacies are inadequately documented in the requirements, the tester must conduct an analysis of them.

Even when detailed requirements are available, the flow and dependency of one requirement to the other is often not immediately apparent. The tester must therefore explore the system in order to gain a sufficient understanding of its behavior to create the most effective test procedures.

---

1. Elfriede Dustin et al., *Automated Software Testing* (Reading, Mass.: Addison-Wesley, 1999), 1-114.

In general, the tester must analyze how any change to any part of the application, such as to a variable or a field, affects the rest of the application. It is not good enough to simply verify aspects of the change itself—for example, that the system allows for the required change, using a subset of input combinations and variations, and that the change is saved correctly; rather, an effective test must also cover all other areas affected by this change.

For example, consider the following requirement statement:

"The system must allow the user to edit the customer name on the customer record screen."

The customer name field and its restrictions are also documented, ideally in the data dictionary. Some testing steps for verifying that the requirement has been met are:

1. Verify that the system allows the user to edit the customer name on the customer-record screen via the user interface, by clicking on the customer record screen and confirming that the customer name can be edited.

2. Try all positive and negative combinations—e.g., all equivalence classes, all boundaries—of customer names allowed. Test a subset of combinations and variations possible within the data dictionary's restrictions.

3. Run a SQL query verifying that the update is saved correctly in the appropriate table(s).

The above steps comprise a good basic test. However, something is missing in order to fully verify this requirement.

Aside from performance and other nonfunctional issues, the question that needs to be answered is, "how is the system otherwise affected when the customer name is changed?" Is there another screen, functionality, or path that uses or is dependent upon the customer name? If so, it will be necessary next to determine how those other parts of the application are affected. Some examples:

- Verify that the "create order" functionality in the order module is now using this changed customer name.

- Add an order record, and verify that the new record has been saved using the new customer name.

- Perform any other possible functions making use of the changed customer name, to verify that it does not adversely affect any other previously working functionality.

Analysis and testing must continue until all affected areas have been identified and tested.

When requirements are not documented in detail, this seemingly simple strategy for effective functional software testing is often overlooked. In fact, in most cases the requirements are not documented in sufficient detail to clearly define relationships between requirements and functional paths, which is critical to test-procedure development. Often, therefore, effective test procedures cannot be designed from the requirements statements alone.

Effective test design includes test procedures that rarely overlap, but instead provide effective coverage with minimal duplication of effort (although duplication sometimes cannot be entirely avoided in assuring complete testing coverage). It is not effective for two test engineers to test the same functionality in two different test procedures, unless this is necessary in order to get the required functional path coverage (as when two paths use duplicate steps at some points).

It is important to analyze test flow to ensure that, during test execution, tests run in proper order, efforts are not unnecessarily duplicated, testers don't invalidate one another's test results, and time is not wasted by producing duplicate or erroneous findings of defects. Such findings can be time consuming for developers to research and for testers to retest, and can skew the defect metrics if not tracked correctly. The test team should review the test plan and design in order to:

- Identify any patterns of similar actions or events used by several transactions. Given this information, test procedures should be developed in a modular fashion so they can be reused and recombined to execute various functional paths, avoiding duplication of test-creation efforts.

- Determine the order or sequence in which specific transactions must be tested to accommodate preconditions necessary to execute a test procedure, such as database configuration, or other requirements that result from control or work flow.

- Create a test procedure relationship matrix that incorporates the flow of the test procedures based on preconditions and postconditions necessary to execute a procedure. A test-procedure relationship diagram that shows the interactions of the various test procedures, such as the high-level test procedure relationship diagram created during test design, can improve the testing effort.

The analyses above help the test team determine the proper sequence of test design and development, so that modular test procedures can be properly linked together and executed in a specific order that ensures contiguous and effective testing.

Another consideration for effectively creating test procedures is to determine and review critical and high-risk requirements, in order to place a greater priority upon, and provide added depth for, testing the most important functions early in the development schedule. It can be a waste of time to invest efforts in creating test procedures that verify functionality rarely executed by the user, while failing to create test procedures for functions that pose high risk or are executed most often. It is imperative that functional test procedure creation be prioritized based on highest-risk and highest-usage functionality. See Item 8 for more detail.

Effective test-case design requires understanding of system variations, flows, and scenarios. It is often difficult to wade through page after page of requirements documents in order to understand connections, flows, and interrelationships. Analytical thinking and attention to detail are required to understand the cause-and-effect connections within the system intricacies. It is insufficient to design and develop high-level test cases that execute the system only at a high level; it is important to also design test procedures at the detailed, gray-box level.

Item 23: Treat Test Procedures As "Living" Documents

Often, test engineers labor to develop test procedures only to execute them once or twice before they become obsolete due to changes in the requirements, design, or implementation. Given the pressures of having to complete the testing, testers continue their tasks without ever revisiting the test procedures. They hope that simply by using intuition and analytical skills they will cover the most important parts of the system. The problems with this type of approach are that if the test procedures become outdated, the initial work creating these tests is wasted, and additional manual tests executed without having a procedure in place cannot be repeated. It is therefore important to treat test procedures as "living" and not static documents, to avoid having them become "shelfware."

Most software projects are developed in an iterative, incremental manner, and test procedures are often developed the same way. It could be counterproductive and infeasible to develop a comprehensive and detailed set of test procedures in the beginning of the project,[1] as the development life cycle brings changes during each iteration. Additionally, time constraints often do not allow the testing team to develop a comprehensive set of test procedures.

In an iterative and incremental development life cycle, numerous software builds are delivered based on a build schedule, and it can be difficult for test-procedure

---

1. The emphasis here is on *detailed* and *comprehensive* test procedures. Design of test procedures should begin as soon as requirements become available, and since requirements are often living documents, it follows that test procedures must be considered living documents as well.

writers to keep up. When the first build is completed and delivered for testing, the expectation is that procedures are available to test it. It doesn't make sense to pursue complete test-procedure development for the entire system if the development team is waiting for a build (a subset of the system) to be tested. In these situations, test procedures must be developed that are targeted for the current build, based on the requirements planned for that build.

It is seldom the case that all requirements, design details, and scenarios are documented and available early in the project; some may not even have been conceptualized yet. Seldom is there one document that lists all functional paths or scenarios of a system. Therefore, test procedures must evolve with each phase of the development process. More details surface during the architecture and design phases, and sometimes even during the implementation phase, as issues are discovered that should have been recognized earlier. Test procedures must be augmented or modified to accommodate this additional information. As requirements change, the testers must be made aware of the changes so they can adjust test procedures accordingly.

System functionality may change or be enhanced during the development life cycle. This may affect several test procedures, which must be redesigned to examine the new functionality. As new functionality becomes available, procedures must be included for testing it.

As defects are found and corrected, test procedures must be updated to reflect the changes and additions to the system. As with new functionality, fixes for defects sometimes change the way the system works. For example, test procedures may have included work-arounds to accommodate a major system bug. Once the fix is in place, the test procedures must be modified to adapt to the change and to verify that the functionality is now implemented correctly.

There may be occasions when testers feel they have had enough time to develop a comprehensive set of test procedures, that there are tests in place for all the known requirements, and that the requirements-to-test traceability matrix is complete. No matter how complete the coverage seems to be, however, with any system of at least moderate complexity, a new test scenario can usually be imagined that hasn't been considered before. The scenarios of how a system can be executed can be endless. Therefore, when a new scenario is encountered, it must be evaluated, assigned a priority, and added to the "living" set of test procedures.

As with any living or evolving document, test procedures should be stored in a version control system.

Item 24: Utilize System Design and Prototypes

P rototypes serve various purposes. They allow users to see the expected result of a feature implementation, providing a preview of the look and feel of the application. They allow users to give feedback on what is being developed, which can be used to revise the prototype and make the final product more acceptable to the user.

Prototypes can be helpful in detecting inconsistencies in requirements. When defining detailed requirements, sometimes contradictions can be hard to spot if they appear in sections many pages apart in one or more documents, or when more than one individual develops or maintains the requirements. Although rigorous approaches and manual inspections can minimize incompleteness and contradictions, there are practical limits to their effectiveness. The creation of a prototype and its design can help in discovering inconsistencies or incompleteness and provide a basis for developing custom tools to uncover any additional issues early in the development process.

Prototyping high-risk and complex areas early allows the appropriate testing mechanism (e.g., a test harness) to be developed and refined early in the process. Attempts to engineer complex testing mechanisms late in the cycle are typically unsuccessful. With a prototype in place early in the development cycle, it is possible to begin defining the outline and approach of the test harness, using the prototype as a model that is one step closer to the actual application.

Designs and prototypes are helpful in refining test procedures, providing a basis for additions and modifications to requirements. They thus become a basis for creating better, more-detailed test procedures. Use of prototypes provides additional information that allows for test-procedure enhancements. Prototypes can provide a level of detail that a static requirements document is unable to provide.

Prototypes are also useful in the design of automated tests using functional testing tools. A prototype can help testers determine where the automated testing tool will run into compatibility issues. This allows time for work-arounds to be investigated and automated test designs to be adjusted prior to the delivery of a software build. Sometimes a prototype can reveal a flaw in the automated testing tool early on, allowing sufficient lead-time to acquire a patch from the tool vendor.

Item 25: Use Proven Testing Techniques when Designing Test-Case Scenarios

tem 10 discusses the importance of planning test data in advance. During the test-design phase, it will become obvious that the combinations and variations of test data that may be used as input to the test procedures can be endless. Since exhaustive testing is usually not possible, it is necessary to use testing techniques that narrow down the number of test cases and scenarios in an effective way, allowing the broadest testing coverage with the least effort. In devising such tests, it's important to understand the available test techniques.

Many books address the various white-box and black-box techniques.[1] While test techniques have been documented in great detail, very few test engineers use a structured test-*design* technique. An understanding of the most widely used test techniques is necessary during test design.

Using a combination of available testing techniques has proven to be more effective than focusing on just one technique. When systems professionals are asked to identify an adequate set of test cases for a program they are testing, they are likely to identify, on average, only about half of the test cases needed for an adequate testing effort. When testers use guesswork to select test cases to execute, there is a high potential for unreliability, including inadequate test coverage.

Among the numerous testing techniques available to narrow down the set of test cases are functional analysis, equivalence partitioning, path analysis,

---

1. For example: Boris Beizer, *Software Testing Techniques* (Hoboken, N.J.: John Wiley & Sons, 1995).

boundary-value analysis, and orthogonal array testing. Here are a few points about each:

- *Functional analysis* is discussed in detail in Item 22. It involves analyzing the expected behavior of the system according to the functional specifications and generating one test procedure or more for each function or feature of the system. If the requirement is that the system provides function x, then the test case(s) must verify that the system provides function x in an adequate manner. One way of conducting functional test analyses is discussed in Item 22. After the functional tests have been defined and numerous testing paths through the application have been derived, additional techniques must be applied to narrow down the inputs for the functional steps to be executed during testing.

- *Equivalence partitioning* identifies ranges of inputs and initial conditions that are expected to produce the same result. Equivalence partitioning relates to the commonality and variances among the different situations in which a system is expected to work. If situations are equivalent, or essentially similar, to one another, it is adequate to test only one of them, not all. Although equivalence is usually intuitively obvious, it is necessary to be careful about what is assumed to be equivalent.

    Consider the following example, which demonstrates equivalence applied to boundaries:

    A password field allows 8 digits; any more are invalid. Since values that are on the same side of a boundary are members of the same "equivalence class," there is no point to testing many members of the same equivalence class (e.g., passwords with 10 digits, 11 digits, 12 digits, etc.), since they will produce the same result.

- *Path analysis* is used to test the internal paths, structure, and connections of a product. It can be applied at two levels. One level is code-based, or **white-box**, testing, and is usually performed during unit test. The **unit test** is done close to the point of creation or modification of the code, usually by the author or programmer. (See Chapter 6 for more detail on unit testing.)

    Path analysis also can be applied at a second level: at the functional or black-box level. The source code may not be available, and black-box testing usually is performed by system testers or user-acceptance testers. Even if the source code is available, testing at the black-box level is performed according

to the specified requirements without evaluating the specifics of their implementation in the source code.

- *Boundary-value (BV) analysis* can complement the path-analysis approach. BV
  testing is used mostly for testing input edit logic. So-called **negative testing**,
  a variation of BV, checks that the processes for filtering out invalid data are
  working acceptably. Boundary conditions should be determined as part of
  designing effective BV test cases, since many defects occur on the boundaries.

  Boundaries define three sets or classes of data: good, bad, and borderline
  (also known as **in-bounds**, **out-of-bounds**, and **on-bounds**).

  As an example, consider an application that checks an input to ensure that
  it is greater than 10.

  - An in-bounds value would be 13, which is greater than 10.

  - An out-of-bounds value would be 5, which is not greater than 10.

  - The value of 10 is actually out-of-bounds, because it is not greater than 10.

In addition to values that lie in or on the boundary, such as endpoints, BV testing uses maximum/minimum values, or more than maximum or minimum,
and one less than maximum and minimum, or zero and null inputs. For
example, when defining the test-input values for a numeric input, one could
consider the following:

- Does the field accept numeric values only, as specified, or does it accept
  alphabetic values?

- What happens if alphabetic values are entered? Does the system accept
  them? If so, does the system produce an error message?

- What happens if the input field accepts characters that are reserved by
  the application or by a particular technology, for example special characters such as ampersands in Web applications? Does the application crash
  when the user inputs these reserved characters?

The system should either not allow out-of-bounds characters to be entered,
or instead should handle them gracefully by displaying an appropriate error
message.

▪ *Orthogonal arrays* allow maximum test coverage from a minimum set of test procedures. They are useful when the amount of potential input data, or combinations of that input data, may be very large, since it is usually not feasible to create test procedures for every possible combination of inputs.[2]

The concept of orthogonal arrays is best presented with an example. Suppose there are three parameters (A, B, and C), each of which has one of three possible values (1, 2, or 3). Testing all possible combinations of the three parameters would require twenty-seven test cases (3^3). Are all twenty-seven of those tests needed? They are if the tester suspects a fault that depends on a specific set of values of all three parameters (a fault, for example, that would occur only for the case when A=1, B=1, *and* C=1). However, it's probably more likely that a fault depends on the values of only two of the parameters. In that case, the fault might occur for each of these three test cases: (A=1, B=1, and C=1); (A=1, B=1, and C=2); and (A=1, B=1, and C=3). Since the value of C in this example appears to be irrelevant to the occurrence of this particular fault, any one of the three tests will suffice. Given that assumption, the following array shows the nine test cases required to catch all such faults:

Case #	A	B	C
1	1	1	3
2	1	2	2
3	1	3	1
4	2	1	2
5	2	2	1
6	2	3	3
7	3	1	1
8	3	2	3
9	3	3	2

The array is orthogonal because for each pair of parameters all combinations of their values occur once. That is, each possible pair of parameters (A and B), (B and C), and (C and A) is shown once. In terms of pairs, it can be said that

---

2. For more on orthogonal arrays, see Elfriede Dustin, "Orthogonally Speaking," *STQE Magazine* 3:5 (Sept.-Oct. 2001). Also available at http://www.effectivesoftwaretesting.com.

this array has a strength of 2. It doesn't have a strength of 3 because not all possible three-way combinations occur— for example, the combination (A=1, B=2, and C=3) doesn't appear. What is important here is that it covers all of the pair-wise possibilities.

It is up to the test designer's judgment to select a representative data sample that truly represents the range of acceptable values. This is sometimes very difficult when there are numerous interrelationships among values. In such cases, the tester may consider adding random samples of possible data sets to the already generated set.

It is generally not possible, feasible, or cost-effective to test a system using all possible permutations of test-parameter combinations. Therefore, it is important to use boundary-value analysis in conjunction with other testing techniques, such as equivalence partitioning and orthogonal arrays, to derive a suitable test data set.

Item 26: Avoid Including Constraints and Detailed Data Elements within Test Procedures

Item 21 discusses the importance of using of a test-procedure template for defining and documenting the test-procedure steps.

The template should be written in a generic manner, to keep it maintainable. It is not good practice to include specific test data in a test procedure, since that would result in unnecessary duplication: For each test data scenario, all test-procedure steps would have to be repeated, with the only changes being the differing data inputs and expected results. Such unnecessary duplication could become a maintenance disaster—for example, were a data element to change, the change would need to be propagated to all test procedures. Consider a Web URL referenced in the documentation for all test procedures. If this URL changes, it must be modified in all of the test-procedure documents—a time-consuming and potentially error-prone task.

To make a test procedure easily maintainable, specific test-data inputs and related expected outputs should be kept in a separate scenario document. Test-data scenario information may be kept in a spreadsheet or database, with each row defining a separate test case. These scenarios can be attached to the test procedure, with example scenarios for each test procedure that feature concrete data. When deriving concrete data, refer to the data dictionary in order to reference data constraints. By helping ensure that test procedures are reusable, these procedures avoid difficult maintenance problems that would be posed were test procedures written using very low-level detail, hard-coded with data that ties the procedures to this specific scenario.

Figure 26.1 provides a simplified example of a test-data scenario spreadsheet used for verifying user IDs and passwords during the system's log-on function.[1] Assume a test procedure exists that documents all the steps necessary for logging on. In the test procedure, the steps will include the data elements—user ID and password. Whenever those data elements are referenced, the tester should refer to the scenario spreadsheet. Note that in actual use, the spreadsheet should include "Actual Outcome" columns (not displayed in Figure 26.1) so testers can document the outcomes during test execution without having to use yet another document.

Test Procedure ID (cross-reference to the test procedure to which this test data relates)			
User ID	**Expected Outcome**	**Password**	**Expected Outcome**
One more digit than allowed—meeting all other constraints	Rejected	One more digit than allowed	Rejected
One less digit than allowed—meeting all other constraints	Accepted	One less digit than allowed	Accepted
Exactly the same number of allowed digits—meeting all other constraints	Accepted	Exactly the number of allowed digits	Accepted
Use combinations of characters that are allowed—meeting all other constraints	Accepted	Use combinations of characters that are allowed	Accepted
Use characters that are not allowed	Rejected	Use characters that are not allowed	Rejected
Use zero input	Rejected	Use zero input	Rejected
Use null input	Rejected	Use null input	Rejected

Figure 26.1 — Example Test-Scenario Spreadsheet

Documenting the test data scenarios described in Figure 26.1 for each separate test procedure would require a huge effort. Keeping the test data in a separate spreadsheet or database, referenced in the main test procedure, allows for easier maintenance and more-effective test documentation.

---

1. Not all possible test data combinations are listed here.

Test-procedure documentation in which data elements are kept outside of the main test procedure, residing instead in a separate location, is especially helpful for automated testing, and can serve as a foundation for other test procedures as well. For both manual and automated test procedures, data elements should be kept separate from their test scripts, using variables instead of hard-coded values within the script, as discussed in Chapter 8.

Item 27: Apply Exploratory Testing

As discussed in Item 22, complete and detailed requirements that define each relationship and dependency are a rarity in today's development environments. A tester is often required to use his analytical skills to determine the intricacies of the application. Sometimes, exploratory testing is required in order to gain knowledge needed for designing effective tests.

The functionality is explored because it is not well understood before testing begins. Exploratory testing is most useful when not much is known about the system under test, such as when the functional specifications are informal or absent, or when there is not enough time to come up with detailed designed and documented test procedures. Exploratory tests can enhance the testing described in Item 22.

Exploratory testing identifies test conditions based on an iterative approach. The pattern of problems found early in exploratory testing helps focus the direction of later test efforts. For example, if an initial investigation indicates that one area of the system is quite buggy while another area is relatively clean, testing is refocused based on this feedback.

Defect-prone areas identified during exploratory testing should be evaluated to determine their correlation to complex areas of the software. Unlike well-thought-out and -planned test procedures, exploratory tests are not defined in advance or carried out precisely according to a plan.

All testing efforts require exploratory testing at one time or another, whether test procedures are based on the most-detailed requirements or no requirements are specified. As testers execute a procedure, discover a bug, and try to recreate and analyze it, some exploratory testing is inevitably performed to help determine the cause. Additionally, during the defect-discovery process, the relationship of a defect to

139

other areas of the application is explored and researched. This usually requires stepping outside the boundaries of the defined test-procedure steps, as all possible test scenarios are rarely documented—it wouldn't be economically feasible to do so.

Another occasion for exploratory testing is when a tester must determine the thresholds (maximums and minimums) of specific features. Consider the following example.

A requirement states: "The field must allow for the creation of pick-list items."

Assuming the data dictionary defines the term "pick-list items" and its associated restrictions and limitations, the tester's first question should be, "How many pick-list items are allowed?" In our example, this question was overlooked during the requirements phase. (Such matters can be missed even during walk-throughs and inspections.)

The tester researches the existing requirements and asks the developers, but the answer is not available. The customer representative has only a vague idea. It becomes necessary for the tester to write and execute a procedure that determines how many pick-list items the field allows. As the tester adds pick-list items, a point comes when the application's performance starts to degrade, or the application simply does not allow the addition of another pick-list item. The tester has now determined the threshold number. After verifying with a customer representative that this number is acceptable, the tester publishes the number for all stakeholders. The tester can now continue executing the original test of the relationship between the field (and its pick-list items) to the application, as described in Item 22.

Exploratory tests cannot be pre-planned, as they are conducted on a case-by-case basis in reaction to encountered conditions. However, it is a good practice to document the exploratory tests before or after execution, adding them to the suite of regression tests (regression testing is discussed in Item 39) for repeatability and reusability and in order to measure adequate coverage.

Exploratory testing "rounds out" the testing effort: It enhances the functional testing described in Item 22, but is not a very powerful technique by itself. Using exploratory testing, often testing coverage cannot be determined or measured, and important functional paths can be missed. It is important that functional-testing procedures be enhanced with new knowledge gained during exploratory testing, treating them as "living documents" as discussed in Item 23.

The most powerful testing effort combines a well-planned, well-defined testing strategy with test cases derived by using functional analysis and such testing techniques as equivalence, boundary testing, and orthogonal-array testing (discussed in Item 25), and is then enhanced with well-thought-out exploratory testing.

There is never enough time in a testing cycle to document all possible test scenarios, variations, and combinations of test procedures. Exploratory testing is a valuable technique for ensuring that most important issues are covered in the testing life cycle.

CHAPTER 6
Unit Testing

U nit testing is the process of exercising an individual portion of code, a **component**, to determine whether it functions properly. Almost all developers perform some level of unit testing before regarding a component or piece of code as complete. Unit testing and integration testing are instrumental for the delivery of a quality software product; yet they are often neglected, or are implemented in a cursory manner.

If unit testing is done properly, later testing phases will be more successful. There is a difference, however, between casual, ad-hoc unit testing based on knowledge of the problem and structured, and repeatable unit testing based on the requirements of the system.

To accomplish structured and repeatable unit testing, executable unit-test software programs must be developed, either prior to or in parallel with development of the software. These test programs exercise the code in ways necessary to verify that it provides the functionality specified by the requirements and that it works as designed. Unit-test programs are considered to be part of the development project, and are updated along with the requirements and source code as the project evolves.

Unit tests ensure that the software meets at least a baseline level of functionality prior to integration and system testing. Discovering defects while a component is still in the development stage offers a significant savings in time and costs: It will not be necessary to place the defect into the defect-tracking system, recreate it, and research it. Rather, it can be fixed in place by one developer prior to release of the software component.

The unit-testing approach discussed here is based on a lightweight, pragmatic method of testing applicable to most software projects. Other, more complicated approaches to unit testing, such as path-coverage analysis, may be necessary for very high-risk systems. However, most projects have neither the time nor the budget to devote to unit testing at that level.

The unit-testing approach covered here differs from **pure unit testing**, the practice of isolating a component from *all* external components that it may call to do its work, allowing the unit to be tested completely on its own. Pure unit testing requires that all underlying components be **stubbed**[1] to provide an isolated environment, which can be very time consuming and carries a high maintenance penalty. Since the unit-testing approach discussed here does not isolate the underlying components from the component under test, this type of unit testing results in some integration testing as well, since the unit under test calls lower-level components while it operates. This approach to unit testing is acceptable only if those underlying components have already been unit tested and proven to work correctly. If this has been done, any unit-test failures are most likely to be in the component under test, not in the lower-level components.

---

1. **Stubbing** is the practice of temporarily creating placeholders for subroutines or other program elements. The stubs return predetermined (hard-wired) results that allow the rest of the program to continue functioning. In this way, program elements can be tested before the logic of all the routines they call has been completed.

Item 28: Structure the Development Approach to Support Effective Unit Testing

S oftware engineers and programmers must be accountable for the quality of their work. Many view themselves as producers of code who are not responsible for testing the code in any formal way; that, in their minds, is the job of the system-testing team. In reality, programmers must be responsible for producing high-quality initial products that adhere to the stated requirements. Releasing code to the testing team when it contains a high number of defects usually results in long correction cycles, most of which can be dramatically reduced through the proper use of unit testing.

Although it is possible that knowledge of the code could lead to less-effective unit tests,[1] this is generally not applicable if the component is performing specific functions related to documented requirements of the system. Even when a component performs only a small part of a functional requirement, it is usually straightforward to determine whether the component fulfills its portion of the requirement properly.

In addition to writing unit-test programs, the developer also must examine code and components with other tools, such as memory-checking software to find

---

1. The author of the code, being thoroughly versed in its inner workings and intended design, may write tests only for scenarios it is likely to pass. Having another person unit test the code introduces a different viewpoint and may catch problems that would not occur to the original author.

145

memory leaks. Having several developers examine the source code and unit-test results may increase the effectiveness of the unit-testing process.

In addition to writing the initial unit test, the developer of the component is in a good position to update the unit test as modifications are made to the code. These modifications could be in response to general improvements and restructuring, a defect, or a requirement change. Making the developer who is responsible for the code also responsible for the unit test is an efficient way to keep unit tests up to date and useful.

Depending on how unit tests are implemented, they could cause the build to halt—making it fail to compile or produce a working executable—if the unit-test program is part of the software build. For example, suppose a developer removes a function, or **method** from a component's C++ interface. If a unit test has not been updated and still requires the presence of this function to compile properly, it will fail to compile. This prevents continuing on to build other components of the system until the unit test is updated. To remedy the problem, the developer must adjust the unit-test program's code to account for the removal of the method from the interface. This example shows why it is important for the developer to perform any necessary updates to the unit test program whenever the code is changed.

Some software projects also require successful unit-test *execution*, not just compilation, for the build to be considered successful. See Item 30 for a discussion of this topic.

Unit tests must be written in an appropriate language capable of testing the code or component in question. For example, if the developer has written a set of pure C++ classes to solve a particular problem or need, the unit test most likely must also be written in C++ in order to exercise the classes. Other types of code, such as COM objects, could be tested using tests written in Visual Basic or possibly with scripts, such as VBScript, JScript, or Perl.

In a large system, code is usually developed in a modular fashion by dividing functionality into several **layers**, each responsible for a certain aspect of the system. For example, a system could be implemented in the following layers:

- **Database abstraction.** An abstraction for database operations **wraps up**[2] database interaction into a set of classes or components (depending on

---

2. **Wrapping up** refers to the practice of putting code or data in one location that is referenced when needed. This way, any changes can be made in that one location, rather than every place where it is used.

the language) that are called by code in other layers to interact with the database.

- **Domain objects.** A set of classes representing entities in the system's problem domain, such as an "account" or an "order," a domain object typically interacts with the database layer. A domain object contains a small amount of code logic, and may be represented by one or more database tables.

- **Business processing.** This refers to components or classes implementing business functionality that makes use of one or more domain objects to accomplish a business goal, such as "place order" or "create customer account."

- **User interface.** The user-visible components of the application that provide a means to interact with the system, this layer can be implemented in a variety of ways. It may be a window with several controls, a Web page, or a simple command-line interface, among other possibilities. The user interface is typically at the "top" of the system's layers.

The above list is a somewhat simplified example of a layered implementation, but it demonstrates the separation of functionality across layers from a "bottom-up" perspective. Each layer consists of several code modules that work together to perform the functionality of the layer.

During the development of such a system, it is usually most effective to assign a given developer to work with a single layer, designing it to communicate with components in other layers via a documented and defined **interface**. In a typical interaction, a user chooses to perform some action via the user interface, and the user-interface (UI) layer calls the business-processing (BP) layer to carry out the action. Internally, the BP layer uses domain objects and other logic to process the request on behalf of the UI layer. During the course of this processing, domain objects will interact with the database-abstraction layer to retrieve or update information in the database. There are many advantageous features in this approach, including the separation of labor across layers, a defined interface for performing work, and the increased potential for reusing layers and code.

Each layer typically includes one or more unit test programs, depending on the size and organization of the layer. In the preceding example, a domain object unit test program would, when executed, attempt to manipulate each domain object just as if the BP layer were manipulating it. For example, the following pseudocode outlines a unit test for a domain-object layer in an order processing system that features three types of elements: "customer," "order," and "item." The unit test attempts to create a customer, an order, and an item, and to manipulate them.

```
// create a test customer, order, and item
try
{
    Customer.Create("Test Customer");
    Order.Create("Test Order 1");
    Item.Create("Test Item 1");
    // add the item to the order
    Order.Add(Item);
    // add the order to the customer
    Customer.Add(Order);
    // remove the order from the customer
    Customer.Remove(Order);
    // delete the customer, order, and item
    Item.Delete();
    Order.Delete();
    Customer.Delete();
}
catch(Error)
{
    // unit test has failed since one of the operations
    // threw an error - return the error
    return Error;
}
```

Similarly, the BP layer includes a unit test that exercises its functionality in the same way that the user interface does, as in the following pseudocode:

```
// place an order
try
{
    OrderProcessingBP.PlaceOrder("New Customer", ItemList);
}
catch(Error)
{
    // unit test has failed since the operation
    // threw an error - return the error
    return Error;
}
```

A natural result of unit testing a layered system without isolating underlying components is some integration testing of the component under test with its associated underlying components, since a higher layer will call the services of a lower layer in order to do its work. In the preceding examples, the BP component uses the customer, order, and item domain objects to implement the place-order functionality. Thus, when the unit test executes the place-order code, it is also indirectly testing the customer, order, and item domain objects. This is a desirable effect of unit testing, since it allows unit-test failures to be isolated to the particular layer in which they occur. For example, suppose the domain objects unit test is successful, but the BP unit test fails. This most likely indicates either an error in the BP logic itself or a problem with the integration between the two layers. Without the domain object unit test, it would be more difficult to tell which layer in fact has a problem.

As mentioned earlier, unit tests should be based on the defined requirements of the system, using use cases or other documentation as guides. A functional requirement typically has implementation support in many layers of the system, each layer adding some piece necessary to satisfying the requirement, as determined during the design phase. Given this multi-layer involvement, each unit test for each affected layer must test the components to make sure they properly implement their pieces of the requirement.

For example, the order-processing system described earlier might have a requirement entitled "Discontinue Item." To satisfy this requirement, the system needs a BP component that can load an item and discontinue it, and can check whether any open orders include this item. This in turn requires that the domain object and database layers allow the item object to be discontinued, perhaps through a discontinue() method, and that the order object support searching for items in the order using an ID. Each layer participates in satisfying the requirement by providing methods or implementations.

Preferably, a representative test for each requirement is included in the unit-test program for each applicable layer, to demonstrate that the layer provides the functionality necessary to satisfy the requirement. Using the previous example, the unit tests for each layer would include a "Test Discontinue Item" method that attempts to test the discontinue-item process against the components whose functionality relates to the requirement.

In addition to testing successful cases of the requirement, **error cases** (also known as **exceptions**) should be tested to verify that the component gracefully handles input errors and other unexpected conditions. For example, a particular requirement states that the user must provide a full name which, as defined in the data dictionary, should not exceed 30 characters. The unit test would try a name of acceptable length, and would also attempt to specify a name of 31 characters, to verify that the component restricts the input to 30 characters or fewer, the boundary specified in the data dictionary.

Item 29: Develop Unit Tests in Parallel or Before the Implementation

Popularized by the development style known as **extreme programming**,[1] the concept of developing unit tests prior to the actual software is useful. Under this approach, requirements guide unit-test development, so they must be defined prior to the development of unit tests. A single requirement usually has implications for many unit tests in the system, which must check the component under test for adherence to the part of the requirement it needs to fulfill. See Item 28 for a discussion of how requirements affect unit testing in a multi-layered system.

There are many benefits to developing unit tests prior to implementing a software component. The first, and most obvious, is that unit testing forces development of the software to be pursued in a way that meets each requirement. The software is considered complete when it provides the functionality required to successfully execute the unit test, and not before; and the requirement is strictly enforced and checked by the unit test. A second benefit is that it focuses the developer's efforts on satisfying the exact problem, rather than developing a larger solution that also happens to satisfy the requirement. This generally results in less code and a more straightforward implementation. A third, more subtle benefit is that the unit test provides a useful reference for determining what the developer

---

1. Generally speaking, **extreme programming** (XP) is a way to develop software. XP changes the way programmers work together. One of the major parts of XP is that programmers work in pairs, and that testing is an intrinsic part of the coding process. For more information, see Kent Beck, *Extreme Programming Explained: Embrace Change* (Boston, Mass.: Addison-Wesley, 2000).

151

intended to accomplish (versus what the requirements state). If there is any question as to the developer's interpretation of the requirements, it will be reflected in the unit test code.

To properly take advantage of this technique, the requirement documentation must for the most part be complete prior to development. This is preferred because developing software prior to the specification of requirements for a particular function can be risky. Requirements should be specified at a somewhat detailed level, so developers can easily determine which objects and functions are required.[2] From the requirement documentation, the developer can lay out a general unit-test strategy for the component, including tests for success and failure.

To ease the development of unit tests, developers should consider an **interface-based** approach to implementing components. It is good software engineering practice to design software around interfaces, rather than around how components function internally. Note that component or software interfaces are not the same as *user interfaces,* which present and retrieve information from the user through graphical or textual means. Component interfaces usually consist of functions that can be called from other components and perform a specific task given a set of input values. If function names, inputs, and outputs are specified and agreed upon, then the implementation of the component may proceed. Designing the interface between components and higher-level functions first allows the developer to design the component from a high level, focusing on its interaction with the outside world. It may also be helpful for the development of the unit test, since the component's interface can be **stubbed**, meaning that each function called by the interface is written to simply return a predetermined, hard-coded result, with no internal logic. For example, consider the following interface:

```
class Order
{
  Create(orderName);
  Delete();
  AddItemToOrder(Item);
}
```

---

2. The RSI (Requirements-Services-Interfaces) approach to use case analysis is an effective way to document requirements from both user and system perspectives. For more information on requirements definition and RSI, see Elfriede Dustin et al., *Quality Web Systems* (Boston, Mass.: Addison-Wesley, 2002), Chapter 2.

The functions referenced in the interface are determined based on requirements that state the system must provide a way to create an order, delete an order, and add items to an order. For writing the unit test, among other purposes, the interface can be stubbed, as in the following example:

```
Create(orderName)
{
    return true;
}
Delete()
{
    return true;
}
AddItemToOrder(Item)
{
    return true;
}
```

The empty functions, or interface stubs, don't actually do anything useful; they simply return "true." The benefit of stubbing a component is that a unit test can be written (and compiled, if necessary) against the interface and will still work properly once the functions are actually implemented.

Unit tests can also assist in the development of the interface itself, since it is useful at times to see how a component will be actually used in code, not just in a design document. Implementing the unit test may lead to refinements and "ease-of-use" enhancements to the component, as the process of implementing code against an interface tends to highlight deficiencies in its design.

In practice, it may be difficult to always create unit tests as the first step. In some situations, parallel development of unit tests and implementation is necessary (and acceptable). There are numerous possible reasons: It may not be immediately obvious how to design the best interface for the component based on the requirements; or the requirements may not be entirely complete, because of outstanding questions or other nonrequirement factors such as time constraints. In such cases, every attempt should still be made to define the component's interface as completely as possible up-front, and to develop a unit test for the known parts of the interface. The remaining portions of the component and the associated unit tests can evolve as development continues on the component.

Updates to the requirements should be handled as follows: First, the unit test is modified with the new requirements, which may require additional functions in the component's interface, or additional values to be taken or returned by the interface. In conjunction with unit-test development, the interface is updated with stubbed implementations of the new parts, to allow the unit test to function. Finally, the component itself is updated to support the new functionality—at which point the developer has an updated component that works with the new requirements, along with an updated unit test.

Item 30: Make Unit-Test Execution Part of the Build Process

Most software systems of significant size are composed of source code that must be built, or **compiled**[1] into executables that can be used by the operating system. A system usually contains many executable files, which may call upon one another to accomplish their work. In a large system, the time it takes to compile the entire code base can be quite significant, stretching into hours or days depending on the capabilities of the hardware performing the build.

In many development environments, each developer must also build a **local version** of the software on the developer's own machine, then make the necessary additions and modifications to implement new functionality. The more code there is to compile, the longer it takes to build—time spent by each developer building each local version of the system. In addition, if there is some defect in a lower layer of the system, the local version may not function properly, which could lead the developer to spend extensive time debugging the local version.

As discussed in Item 29, unit-test programs are valuable for ensuring that the software functions as specified by the requirements. Unit-test programs can also be used to verify that the latest version of a software component functions as expected, prior to compiling other components that depend on it. This eliminates wasted build time, while also allowing developers to pinpoint which component of the system has failed and start immediately investigating that component.

---

1. In most development environments, the term **compiling** describes the act of producing an executable module from a set of source-code files, such as a collection of C++ files.

In a layered software architecture, as described in Item 28, layers build upon each other, with higher layers calling down to lower layers to accomplish a goal and satisfy a requirement. Compiling a layered system requires that each lower layer be present—compiled and ready for use—for the next-higher layer to successfully compile and run. This kind of bottom-up build process is common, and allows for reuse of layers, as well as separation of responsibilities among developers.

If unit tests have been written for the components in each layer, it is usually possible for the build environment to automatically execute the unit-test programs after the build of a layer is finished. This could be done in a make-file or a post-build step, for example. If the unit test executes successfully, meaning that no errors or failures are detected in the layer's components, the build continues to the next layer. If the unit test fails, however, the build stops at the layer that failed. Tying a successful build to successful unit-test execution can avoid a lot of wasted compiling and debugging time, while ensuring that the unit tests are actually executed.

It is quite common that unit tests are not updated, maintained, and executed on a regular basis after they are written. Requiring each build to also execute the associated unit tests avoids these problems. This comes with a price, however. When project schedules are tight, especially during bug-fix and testing cycles, there can be considerable pressure to turn fixes around very quickly, sometimes in a period of minutes. Updating the unit-test programs to allow the layer to build can seem like a nuisance, even a waste of time at that particular moment. It is important to keep in mind, however, that the minimal time spent updating a unit test can prevent hours of debugging and searching for defects later. This is especially important if pressure is high and source code is being modified at a fast pace.

Many development projects use **automated builds** to produce regular releases of systems, sometimes on a nightly basis, that include the latest changes to the code. In an automated-build situation, the failure of a component to compile properly halts the build until someone can rectify the issue with the source code. This is, of course, unavoidable, since a syntactical error in the source code must be examined and corrected by a developer in order for the build to proceed.

Adding automated unit-test execution to the build adds another dimension of quality to the build, beyond simply having a system that is syntactically correct and therefore compiles. It ensures that the product of an automated build is in fact a successfully unit-tested system. The software is always in a testable state, and does not contain major errors in the components that can be caught by the unit tests.

A major issue in unit testing is inconsistency. Many software engineers fail to employ a uniform, structured approach to unit testing. Standardizing and streamlining unit tests can reduce their development time and avoid differences in the way they are used. This is especially important if they are part of the build process, since it is easier to manage unit-test programs if they all behave the same way. For example, unit-test behavior when encountering errors or processing command-line arguments should be predictable. Employing standards for unit tests, such as that unit-test programs all return *zero* for success and *one* for failure, leads to results that can be picked up by the build environment and used as a basis for deciding whether the build should continue. If no standard is in place, different developers will probably use different return values, thus complicating the situation.

One way to achieve such standardization is to create a **unit-test framework**. This is a system that handles processing of command-line arguments (if any) and reporting of errors. Typically, a framework is configured at startup with a list of tests to run, and then calls them in sequence. For example:

```
Framework.AddTest(CreateOrderTest)
Framework.AddTest(CreateCustomerTest)
Framework.AddTest(CreateItemTest)
```

Each test (i.e., CreateOrderTest, CreateCustomerTest, and CreateItemTest) is a function somewhere in the unit-test program. The framework executes all of these tests by calling these functions one by one, and handles any errors they report, as well as returning the result of the unit test as whole, usually **pass** or **fail**. A framework can reduce unit-test development time, since only the individual tests need be written and maintained in each layer, not all of the supporting error-handling and other execution logic. The common unit-test functions are written only one time, in the framework itself. Each unit-test program simply implements the test functions, deferring to the framework code for all other functionality, such as error handling and command-line processing.

Since unit-test programs are directly related to the source code they test, each should reside in the project or workspace of its related source code. This allows for effective configuration management of the unit tests with the components being tested, avoiding "out-of-sync" problems. The unit tests are so dependent upon the underlying components that it is very difficult to manage them any way other than as part of the layer. Having them reside in the same workspace or project also makes it easier to automatically execute them at the end of each build.

The reusable portions of a unit-testing framework, however, can exist elsewhere, and simply be called by each unit-test program as needed.

CHAPTER 7
Automated Testing Tools

A utomated testing tools can enhance the testing effort—as long as expectations are managed, tool issues are understood, and a tool compatible with the system-engineering environment is selected. It is also important that the tool match the task at hand, and that the tests lend themselves to automation. Many types of testing tools are available for use throughout the various development life cycle phases, including the highly touted capture/playback testing tools.

Sometimes it is determined after research and evaluation that no tool available on the market completely suits the project's needs. In that case, it is necessary to decide whether to develop a unique solution, in the form of scripts or custom tools, or to rely solely on manual testing.

In other cases, there may be commercially available tools that would work for the testing effort, but offer more features than are needed, adding significant cost. This is another situation in which building a custom tool may be reasonable. However, careful analysis is required to verify that building the tool will not be more expensive in the long run than buying it.

There are also situations that mandate a custom-built tool, especially if a particular system component poses a high risk, or is proprietary and cannot be tested by an off-the-shelf tool.

In some cases, particularly when investing large amounts of money in automated testing tools, the needs of the entire organization must be considered. The tool that is selected or built must work properly with the selected technologies, and must fit into the project's budget and time frame allowed for introducing a tool.

Evaluation criteria must be established, and the tool's capabilities must be verified according to those criteria prior to purchase.

Examining these issues early in the life-cycle will avoid costly changes later.

Item 31: Know the Different Types of Testing-Support Tools[1]

While functional testing tools (also called "capture/playback tools") are much hyped in the testing industry, it is important to be aware of the other types of tools available to support the testing life cycle. This item provides an overview of the available tools, listed in Table 31.1, that support the various testing phases. Although other tools, such as defect-tracking tools and configuration-management tools, are also used in most software projects, the table lists only tools specific to test automation.

All of the tools listed in Table 31.1 may be valuable for improving the testing life cycle. However, before an organization can decide which tools to purchase, an analysis must be conducted to determine which of the tools, if any, will be most beneficial for a particular testing process. The capabilities and drawbacks of a tool are examined by comparing the current issues to be solved with a target solution, evaluating the potential for improvement, and conducting a cost/benefit analysis. Before purchasing any tool to support a software engineering activity, such an evaluation should be performed, similar to the automated test tool evaluation process described in Item 34.

---

1. Adapted from Elfriede Dustin et al., *Automated Software Testing* (Reading, Mass.: Addison-Wesley, 1999), Section 3.2.

Table 31.1. Test Tools

Type of Tool	Description
Test-Procedure Generators	Generate test procedures from requirements/design/object models
Code (Test) Coverage Analyzers and Code Instrumentors	Identify untested code and support dynamic testing
Memory-Leak Detection	Verify that an application is properly managing its memory resources
Metrics-Reporting Tools	Read source code and display metrics information, such as complexity of data flow, data structure, and control flow. Can provide metrics about code size in terms of numbers of modules, operands, operators, and lines of code.
Usability-Measurement Tools	User profiling, task analysis, prototyping, and user walk-throughs
Test-Data Generators	Generate test data
Test-Management Tools	Provide such test-management functions as test-procedure documentation and storage and traceability
Network-Testing Tools	Monitoring, measuring, testing, and diagnosing performance across entire network
GUI-Testing Tools (Capture/Playback)	Automate GUI tests by recording user interactions with online systems, so they may be replayed automatically
Load, Performance, and Stress Testing Tools	Load/performance and stress testing
Specialized Tools	Architecture-specific tools that provide specialized testing of specific architectures or technologies, such as embedded systems

Following are some key points regarding the various types of testing tools.

- *Test-procedure generators.* A requirements-management tool may be coupled with a specification-based test-procedure (case) generator. The requirements-management tool is used to capture requirements information, which is then processed by the test-procedure generator. The generator creates test procedures by statistical, algorithmic, or heuristic means. In statistical test-procedure generation, the tool chooses input structures and values in a statistically random distribution, or a distribution that matches the usage profile of the software under test.

Most often, test-procedure generators employ action, data, logic, event, and state-driven strategies. Each of these strategies is employed to probe for a different kind of software defect. When generating test procedures by heuristic or failure-directed means, the tool uses information provided by the test engineer. Failures the test engineer has discovered frequently in the past are entered into the tool. The tool then becomes knowledge-based, using the knowledge of historical failures to generate test procedures.

- *Code-coverage analyzers and code instrumentors.* Measuring structural coverage enables the development and test teams to gain insight into the effectiveness of tests and test suites. Tools in this category can quantify the complexity of the design, measure the number of integration tests required to qualify the design, help produce the integration tests, and measure the number of integration tests that have not been executed. Other tools measure multiple levels of test coverage, including segment, branch, and conditional coverage. The appropriate level of test coverage depends upon the criticality of a particular application.

    For example, an entire test suite can be run through a code-coverage tool to measure branch coverage. The missing coverage of branches and logic can then be added to the test suite.

- *Memory-leak detection tools.* Tools in this category are used for a specific purpose: to verify that an application is properly using its memory resources. These tools ascertain whether an application is failing to release memory allocated to it, and provide runtime error detection. Since memory issues are involved in many program defects, including performance problems, it is worthwhile to test an application's memory usage frequently.

- *Usability-measurement tools.* Usability engineering is a wide-ranging discipline that includes user-interface design, graphics design, ergonomic concerns, human factors, ethnography, and industrial and cognitive psychology. Usability testing is largely a manual process of determining the ease of use and other characteristics of a system's interface. However, some automated tools can assist with this process, although they should never replace human verification of the interface.[2]

- *Test-data generators.* Test-data generators aid the testing process by automatically generating the test data. Many tools on the market support the generation of test data and populating of databases. Test-data generators can populate a database quickly based on a set of rules, whether data is needed for functional testing, data-driven load testing, or performance and stress testing.

- *Test-management tools.* Test-management tools support the planning, management, and analysis of all aspects of the testing life cycle. Some test-management tools, such as Rational's TestStudio, are integrated with requirement and configuration management and defect tracking tools, in order to simplify the entire testing life cycle.

- *Network-testing tools.* The popularity of applications operating in client-server or Web environments introduces new complexity to the testing effort. The test engineer no longer exercises a single, closed application operating on a single system, as in the past. Client-server architecture involves three separate components: the server, the client, and the network. Inter-platform connectivity increases potential for errors. As a result, the testing process must cover the performance of the server and the network, the overall system performance, and functionality across the three components. Many network test tools allow the test engineer to monitor, measure, test, and diagnose performance across an entire network.

- GUI-testing tools (capture/playback tools). Many automated GUI testing tools are on the market. These tools usually include a record-and-playback feature, which allows the test engineer to create (record), modify, and run (play back) automated tests across many environments. Tools that record the GUI components at the user-interface control, or "widget," level (not the bitmap level) are most useful. The record activity captures the keystrokes entered by the test engineer, automatically creating a script in a high-level language in the background. This recording is a computer program, referred to as a test script. Using only the capture and playback features of such a tool uses only about one-tenth of its capacity, however. To get the best value from a capture/playback tool, engineers

---

2. Elfriede Dustin et al., "Usability," Chapter 7.5 in *Quality Web Systems: Performance, Security, and Usability* (Boston, Mass.: Addison-Wesley, 2002).

should take advantage of the tool's built-in scripting language. See Item 36 for more on why not to rely on capture/playback alone.

The recorded script must be modified by the test engineer to create a reusable and maintainable test procedure. The outcome of the script becomes the baseline test. The script can then be played back on a new software build to compare its results to the baseline.

A test tool that provides recording capability is usually bundled with a comparator, which automatically compares actual outputs with expected outputs and logs the results. The results can be compared pixel-by-pixel, character-by-character, or property-by-property, depending on the test comparison type, and the tool automatically pinpoints the difference between the expected and actual result. For example, Rational Robot and Mercury's Winrunner log a positive result in the test log as a pass and depict it on the screen in green, while a negative result is represented in red.

- *Load, performance, and stress testing tools.* Performance-testing tools allow the tester to examine the response time and load capabilities of a system or application. The tools can be programmed to run on a number of client machines simultaneously to measure a client-server system's response times when it is accessed by many users at once. Stress testing involves running the client machines in high-stress scenarios to determine whether and when they break.

- *Specialized tools.* Different application types and architectures will require specialized testing of architecturally specific areas. For example, a Web application will require automated link testers to verify that there are no broken links, and security test programs to check the Web servers for security related problems.

Item 32: Consider Building a Tool Instead of Buying One

Suppose a testing team has automated 40 percent of the testing for a project using an off-the-shelf capture/playback tool, only to realize that adequate testing coverage cannot be achieved by using this tool. In situations like these, in addition to asking the development team to add **testability hooks** (code inserted into the program specifically to facilitate testing), the team must consider building a new automated testing "tool" that enhances the capture/playback tool's reach.

Inadequacy of the testing tool is not the only reason why this type of automated testing might be insufficient. Sometimes the application may not lend itself to automation using a capture/playback tool, either because there is no compatible tool on the market, or because the task at hand is too complex for the capture/playback tool to handle. These, too, are cases requiring custom solutions.

Whether to buy or build a tool requires management commitment, including budget and resource approvals. The course of action must be carefully evaluated: Pros and cons of building versus buying must be weighed. Initially, it might seem easier and cheaper to simply build a tool rather than buying one, but building a tool from scratch can be just as expensive, or even more expensive, than buying one, since the custom tool itself must be tested and maintained.

Nonetheless, there are certain situations that offer no other choice than to build the tool:

- *Operating system incompatibility.* If the tool-evaluation suggestions in Item 34 have been followed and it has been determined that no tool currently on the market is compatible with the various operation systems in use, there is no

167

other choice than to consider building a custom tool that will work in the specific environment under test.

- *Application incompatibility.* The application under test may contain an element, such as a third-party add-on, known to cause compatibility problems with any capture/playback tool on the market. If a work-around cannot be created, it may not be possible to use the capture/playback tool. Even if a work-around can be created, it may not be worth the effort; instead of investing money in a capture/playback tool that is not 100-percent compatible with the application under test and devoting further resources to creating a work-around solution, it may be more beneficial to create a home-grown set of testing scripts or other custom tool.

- *Specialized testing needs.* For the most efficient testing, specialized, automated testing scripts are often required to augment formal, vendor-provided tool-based testing. Often a test harness must be developed as an enhancement to the GUI testing tool, to cover the automated testing for a complex, critical component that the GUI testing tool cannot reach.

If the decision is made to build a tool, there are important steps to follow. Assuming the task at hand is understood and the tests lend themselves to this type of automation, these steps include:

- Determine the resources, budgets, and schedules required for building the testing tool well in advance.

- Get buy-in and approval from management for this effort.

- Treat the development of the testing tool as a part of the software-development effort.

- Manage the tool's source code in version control with the rest of system. If the tool isn't versioned, it will easily fall out of sync with the software and cease to function properly.

- Treat the development of the testing tool as a main objective. When building a tool is treated as a side project, it seldom is pursued with all of the best development practices that are important for producing a solid piece of software—and the tool itself may contain bugs or be difficult to implement and maintain.

- As with any piece of code, test the home-grown testing tool itself to verify that it works according to its requirements. It is critical that a testing tool not produce false negatives or false positives.

The process of building a tool can range from writing a simple batch file or Perl script to creating a complex C++ application. The appropriate language with which to build the tool depends on the task at hand and the function of the test. For example, if the function of the test is to thoroughly exercise a complex C++ calculation DLL using some or all of its possible inputs, a suitable solution may be another C++ program that directly calls the DLL, supplying the necessary combinations of test values and examining the results.

In addition to exploring testing tools on the market and considering building custom tools, it may also be worthwhile to investigate the many free or shareware tools available on the Internet. Some are dedicated testing tools, such as DejaGNU, TETware, xUnit, and Microsoft's Web Application Stress Tool (WAST), while others, such as macro-recorders, XML editors, and specialized scripting tools, are not designed specifically for testing but may be useful in certain situations.

Finally, major tool vendors often offer lower-priced "light" (less-capable) versions of their tools, in addition to their major line of tools. For example, Mercury offers the Astra line, Rational offers Visual Test, and Watchfire offers the Linkbot Personal Edition. These simplified versions may be sufficient for certain testing efforts, when the budget doesn't allow purchasing the more-expensive, more-powerful tools.

Item 33: Know the Impact of Automated Tools on the Testing Effort[1]

utomated testing tools are merely a part of the solution—they aren't a magic answer to the testing problem. Automated testing tools will never replace the analytical skills required to conduct testing, nor will they replace manual testing. Automated testing must be seen as an enhancement to the manual-testing process.

Along with the idea of automated testing come high expectations. A lot is demanded of technology and automation. Some people have the notion that an automated test tool should be able to accomplish everything from test planning to test execution, without much manual intervention. While it would be great if such a tool existed, there is no such capability on the market today. Others wrongly believe that it takes only one test tool to support all test requirements, regardless of environment parameters such as operating system or programming language. However, environment factors do put limits on manual and automated testing efforts.

Some may incorrectly assume that an automated test tool will immediately reduce the test effort and schedule. While automated testing is of proven value and can produce a return on investment, there isn't always an immediate payback. Sometimes an automation effort might fail, because of unrealistic expectations, incorrect implementation, or selection of the wrong tool.

---

1. Adapted from Elfriede Dustin et al., *Automated Software Testing* (Reading, Mass.: Addison-Wesley, 1999), Chapter 2.

The following list corrects some common misconceptions about automated testing that persist in the software industry, and provides guidelines for avoiding the automated-testing euphoria.

- *Multiple tools are often required.* Generally, a single test tool will not fulfill all the automated testing requirements for an organization, unless that organization works only with one type of operating system and one type of application. Expectations must to be managed. It must be made clear that currently there exists no one single tool on the market that is compatible with all operating systems and programming languages.

  This is only one reason why several tools are required to test the various technologies. For example, some tools have problems recognizing third-party user-interface controls. There are hundreds of third-party add-on controls available with which a developer could implement an application. A tool vendor might claim to be compatible with the main language in which the application is developed, but it is not possible to know whether the tool is compatible with all of the third-party add-ons that may be in use, unless the vendor specifically claims compatibility with them all. It's almost impossible to create a single test tool that is compatible with all third-party add-ons.

  If a testing tool is already owned but the system architecture has not yet been developed, the test engineer can give the developers a list of third-party controls that are supported by the test tool. See Item 34 for a discussion on efficiently evaluating a tool and purchasing the correct tool for the development environment.

- *Test effort does not decrease.* A primary impetus for introducing an automated test tool in a project may be the hope of reducing the testing effort. Experience has shown that a learning curve is associated with attempts to apply automated testing to a new project. Test-effort savings do not necessarily come immediately. The first time through, it takes more effort to record the scripts and then edit them to create maintainable and repeatable tests than it would to just execute their steps manually. However, some test or project managers who may have read only the test-tool literature may be over-anxious to realize the potential of the automated tools more rapidly than is feasible.

  Surprising as it may seem, there is a good chance that the test effort will initially *increase* when an automated test tool is first brought in. Introducing an automated test tool to a new project adds a whole new level of complexity to the test program. And, in addition to accounting for the learning curve for the test engineers to become proficient in the use of the automated tool, managers must not forget that no tool will eliminate *all* need for manual testing in a project.

- *Test schedules do not decrease.* A related misconception about automated testing is that the introduction of an automated testing tool on a new project will immediately reduce the test schedule. Since the testing effort actually increases when an automated test tool is initially introduced, the testing schedule cannot be expected to decrease at first; rather, allowance must be made for schedule increases. After all, the current testing process must be augmented, or an entirely new testing process must be developed and implemented, to allow for the use of automated testing tools. An automated testing tool will provide additional testing coverage, but it will not generate immediate schedule reductions.

- *Automated testing follows the software development life cycle.* Initial introduction of automated testing requires careful analysis of the application under test to determine which sections of the application can be automated. It also requires careful attention to procedure design and development. The automated test effort can be viewed as having its own mini-development life cycle, complete with the planning and coordination issues attendant to any development effort.

- *A somewhat stable application is required.* An application must be somewhat stable in order to automate it effectively using a capture/playback tool. Often, it is infeasible or not possible for maintenance reasons, to automate against portions of the software that keep changing. Sometimes automated tests cannot be executed in their entirety, but must be executed only partway through, because of problems with the application.

- *Not all tests should be automated.* As previously mentioned, automated testing is an enhancement to manual testing, but it can't be expected that all tests on a project can be automated. It is important to analyze which tests lend themselves to automation. Some tests are impossible to automate, such as verifying a printout. The test engineer can automatically send a document to the printer —a message can even pop up that says, "printed successfully"—but the tester must verify the results by physically walking over to the printer to make sure the document really printed. (The printer could have been off line or out of paper. The printout could be misaligned, or data elements could be cut off at the edges.) Then, the actual content printed on the paper must be verified visually. Chapter 5 discusses which tests to automate.

- *A test tool will not allow for automation of every possible test combination.* A commonly-believed fallacy is that a test tool can automate 100 percent of the requirements of any given test effort. Given an endless number of permutations and combinations of system and user actions possible with modern applications, there is not enough time to test every possibility, no matter how sophisticated the automated testing tool is.

  Even if it were theoretically possible, no test team has enough time or resources to support 100-percent automation of all testing for an entire application.

- *The tool's entire cost includes more than its shelf price.* Implementation of automated testing incurs not only the tool's purchase cost, but also training costs, costs of automated script development, and maintenance costs.

- *"Out-of-the-box" automation is not efficient.* Many tool vendors try to sell their products by exaggerating the tool's ease of use. They overlook any learning curve associated with the use of the new tool. Vendors are quick to point out that the tool can simply capture (record) a test engineer's keystrokes and create a script in the background, which can then simply be played back. But effective automation is not that simple. Test scripts generated by the tool during recording must be modified manually, requiring tool-scripting knowledge, in order to make the scripts robust, reusable, and maintainable.

- *Training is required.* Sometimes a tester is handed a new testing tool only to have it to end up on the shelf or be implemented inefficiently, because the tester hasn't had any training in using the tool. When introducing an automated tool to a new project, it's important that tool training be incorporated early in the schedule and regarded as one of the important milestones. Since testing occurs throughout the system development life cycle, tool training should occur early in the cycle. This ensures that the automated-testing tool can be applied to earlier as well as later testing phases, and that tool issues can be brought up and resolved early. In this way, testability and automation capabilities can be built into the system under test from the start.

  Sometimes tool training is initiated too late in a project to be useful. Often, for example, only the capture/playback portion of the testing tool ends up being used, so scripts have to be repeatedly re-created, causing much wasted effort. Early training in use of the tool would eliminate much of this work.

- *Testing tools can be intrusive.* Some testing tools are intrusive; for the automated tool to work correctly, it may be necessary to insert special code into the application to integrate with the testing tool. Development engineers may be reluctant to incorporate this extra code. They may fear it will cause the system to operate improperly or require complicated adjustments to make it work properly.

  To avoid such conflicts, the test engineers should involve the development staff in selecting an automated tool. If the tool requires code additions (not all tools do), developers need to know that well in advance. To help reassure developers that the tool will not cause problems, they can be offered feedback from other companies that have experience using the tool, and can be shown documented vendor claims to that effect.

  Intrusive tools pose the risk that defects introduced by the testing hooks (code inserted specifically to facilitate testing) and instrumentation could interfere with the normal functioning of the system. Regression tests on the production-ready, cleaned-up code may be required to ensure that there are no tool-related defects.

- *Testing tools can be unpredictable.* As with all technologies, testing tools can be unpredictable. For example, repositories may become corrupt, baselines may not be restored, or tools may not always behave as expected. Often, much time must be spent tracking down the problem or restoring a back-up of a corrupted repository. Testing tools are also complex applications in themselves, so they may have defects that interfere with the testing effort and may require vendor-provided patches. All of these factors can consume additional time during automated testing.

- *Automaters may lose sight of the testing goal.* Often, when a new tool is used for the first time in a testing program, more time is spent on automating test scripts than on actual testing. Test engineers may become eager to develop elaborate automation scripts, losing sight of the real goal: to test the application. They must keep in mind that automating test scripts is *part* of the testing effort, but doesn't replace it. Not everything can or should be automated. As previously mentioned, it's important to evaluate which tests lend themselves to automation.

When planning an automated testing process, it's important to clearly define the division of duties. It's not necessary for the entire testing team to spend its time automating scripts; only some of the test engineers should spend their time automating scripts. The engineers selected for this work should have backgrounds in software development.

Item 34: Focus on the Needs of Your Organization

Anyone participating in test engineer user-group discussions[1] will frequently encounter the following questions: "Which testing tool is the best on the market? Which do you recommend?"

Users will respond with as many different opinions as there are contributors to the testing forum. Often a user most experienced with a particular tool will argue that that specific tool is the best solution.

However, the most useful answer to this popular question is: "It depends." Which testing tool is best depends on the needs of the organization and the system-engineering environment—as well on as the testing methodology, which will, in part, dictate how automation fits into the testing effort.

Following is a list of best practices to consider when choosing a testing tool:[2]

- *Decide on the type of testing life-cycle tool needed.* If the automation task is an organization-wide effort, gather input from all stakeholders. What do they want the automation to accomplish? For example, it may be that in-house users of the system under test would like to use the tool for user-acceptance testing. Determine what is expected from automation, so those expectations can be managed early on, as discussed in Item 33.

---

1. Two good examples of such discussions are the Web site http://www.qaforums.com and the Usenet newsgroup comp.software.testing.

2. For additional information on tool evaluation, see Elfriede Dustin et al., *Automated Software Testing* (Reading, Mass.: Addison-Wesley, 1999), 67–103.

Sometimes a test manager is instructed to find a tool that supports most of the organization's testing requirements, if feasible. Such a decision requires considering the systems-engineering environment and other organizational needs as well as developing a list of tool-evaluation criteria. What does the system-engineering environment look like? What application development technologies are in use? These questions should be part of the tool-selection process, feeding into the development of evaluation criteria.

Other times, testers may be instructed to look for a testing tool to support the specific project they are working on, such as a Web project requiring Web-testing tools, while the organization as a whole produces desktop or client-server applications. It is best not to limit the automated test tool selection criteria to one single project, because obtaining such a tool may be an investment good for only that project, with the test tool becoming "shelfware" after the immediate project has been completed.

Once the type of testing tool has been decided on, criteria can be further defined. For example, if a tool is to be used across an entire organization, the test engineer must make sure it is compatible with as many operating systems, programming languages, and other aspects of the organization's technical environment as possible. The test engineer must review the organization's system-engineering environment by addressing the questions and concerns specified in this chapter and documenting the findings.

- *Identify the various system architectures.* During the survey of the system-engineering environment, the test engineer must identify the technical application architecture, including middleware, databases, and operating systems most commonly used within the organization or the particular project. The test engineer also must identify the languages used to develop the GUI for each application, along with all third-party add-ons used. Additionally, the test engineer must gain an understanding of the detailed architecture design, which can influence performance requirements. A review of prevalent performance requirements, including performance under heavy loads, intricate security mechanisms, and measures of availability and reliability for a system, is beneficial.

  The specific selection criteria on any given effort will depend on the applicable system requirements of the applications under test. If it is not possible to use particular automated test tools across several projects or applications, then it might be necessary to develop the selection criteria relative to the most significant applications under test within the organization.

- *Determine whether more than one tool is required.* The test team responsible for implementing a test tool must be sure to include its own expectations in the selection criteria. As mentioned in Item 32, a single tool generally cannot satisfy all test-tool interests and requirements within an organization. The tool chosen should at a minimum satisfy the more-immediate requirements. As the automated test-tool industry continues to evolve and grow, test-tool coverage of system requirements is likely to expand, and the chances may improve for a single tool to provide most of the functionality desired. Eventually, one tool may be ideal for most GUI testing; another tool may cover the bulk of performance testing; and a third tool may do most of what's needed for usability testing. For now, multiple test tools must be considered, depending on the testing phase, and expectations regarding the tools' capabilities must be managed.

  It may be that no single tool is compatible with all operating systems and programming languages in a given environment. For example, when testing a LINUX client connecting to an IBM mainframe using 3270 sessions and a Java client, it will be difficult to find a tool that does LINUX, Java, and 3270 terminal emulation. More often, several tools are required to test the various technologies. In some cases, no tool on the market is compatible with the target environment, and it will be necessary to develop a custom automated-testing solution. Vendor-provided automated testing tools may have to be excluded from the test strategy in favor of a tool or test harness developed in-house. (For discussion of developing test harnesses, see Item 37.)

- *Understand how data is managed by the applications(s) under test.* The test team must understand the data managed by the target applications and define how the automated test tool supports data verification. A primary purpose of most applications is to transform data into meaningful information and present it to the user in graphical or text form. The test team must understand how this transformation is to be performed by the application so that test strategies can be defined to verify the correctness of the transformation.

- *Review help-desk problem reports.* When an application, or version of an application, is in operation, the test team can monitor help-desk trouble reports in order to study the most prevalent problems reported by users of the application. If a new version of the application is being developed, the test team can focus the testing effort on the most frequently reported problems of the operational system, including identifying a test tool that supports this area of testing, among other criteria.

- *Know the types of tests to be developed.* Since there are many types of test phases for any given project, it is necessary to select the types of testing of interest. The test strategy should be defined at this point so the test team can review the types of tests needed—regression testing, stress or volume testing, usability testing, and so forth. Questions to ask to help determine types of tests to employ include: What is the most important feature needed in a tool? Will the tool be used mainly for stress testing? Some test tools specialize in **source code coverage analysis**. That is, they identify all of the possible source-code paths that must be verified through testing. Is this capability required for the particular project or set of projects? Other test-tool applications to consider include those that support process automation and bulk data loading through input files. Consider what the test team hopes to accomplish with the test tool. What is the goal? What functionality is desired?

- *Know the schedule.* Another concern when selecting a test tool is its fit with and impact upon the project schedule. It is important to review whether there will be enough time for the necessary testers to learn the tool within the constraints of the schedule. When there is not enough time in the project schedule, it may be advisable not to introduce an automated test tool. By postponing the introduction of a test tool to a more opportune time, the test team may avoid the risk of rushing the introduction, perhaps selecting the wrong tool for the organization. In either case, the test tool likely will not be well received, and those who might otherwise become champions for automated testing may instead become the biggest opponents of such tools.

- *Know the budget.* Once the type of tool required has been determined, it may be tempting to go after the best of the breed. However, it is important to take into account the available budget. It's possible to spend months evaluating the most powerful tool, only to find out that its costs exceeds the budget. Additionally, a budget might be needed for training to bring people up to speed on the tool, or additional staffing resources may be required if there is no developer on the testing team.

Most importantly, testers should remember that there is no one best tool for all environments out there on the market. All tools have their pros and cons for different environments. Which tool is the best depends on the system-engineering environment and other organizational specific requirements and criteria.

Item 35: Test the Tools on an Application Prototype

Given the broad spectrum of technologies used in software development, it is important to verify that testing-tool candidates function properly with the system being developed. The best way to accomplish this is to have the vendor demonstrate the tool on the application being tested. However, this usually is not possible, since the system under test is often not yet available during the tool-evaluation phase.

As an alternative, the development staff can create a system prototype for evaluating a set of testing tools. During the evaluation, it may be discovered that some tools function abnormally with the selected development technologies—for example, that the test team cannot properly operate the capture/playback or other important features of the tool.

Early in the development of the system, the prototype must be based on certain key areas of the system that will provide a somewhat representative sample of the technologies to be used in the system. The performance of tool-compatibility tests is especially important for GUI-test tools, because such tools may have difficulty recognizing custom controls in the application's user interface. Problems are often encountered with the calendars, grids, and spin controls that are incorporated into many applications, especially on Windows platforms. These controls, or widgets, were once called VBXs, then OCXs, and now are referred to as Active-X Controls in the Windows and Web interface worlds. They are usually written by third parties, and few test tool manufacturers can keep up with the hundreds of controls created by the various companies.

As an example of this problem, a test tool may be compatible with all releases of Visual Basic and PowerBuilder used to build the application under test; but if an incompatible third-party custom control is introduced into the application, the tool might not recognize the object on the screen. It may even be that most of the application uses a third-party grid that the test tool does not recognize. The test engineer must decide whether to automate testing of the unrecognized parts via a work-around solution, or to test these controls manually.

Such incompatibility issues may be circumvented if the test engineer evaluates and chooses the appropriate tool to match the project's needs right from the start.

The staff member evaluating test tools must also have the appropriate background. Usually, a technical background is required to ensure that the engineer can use the tool against the application, or a prototype, in such a way as to guarantee that it functions properly with the required technologies. Moreover, ease-of-use, flexibility, and the other characteristics discussed in Item 34 are best evaluated by a technical staff member.

There is no substitute for seeing a tool in action against a prototype of the proposed application. Any vendor can promise tool compatibility with many Web application technologies; but it is best to verify that claim. With the pace of technology "churn" in the software industry, no vendor exists that can claim compatibility with all technologies. It's up to each organization to ensure that the selected tool or tools meet its needs.

CHAPTER 8

Automated Testing: Selected Best Practices

To be most effective, automated software testing should be treated as a software development project. Like software application development, the test development effort requires careful analysis and design based on detailed requirements. This section covers using selected automated testing best practices—for example, how best to apply capture/playback technologies in a testing effort, and the pitfalls associated with using this type of automation technique. Automating regression tests, automated software builds, and smoke tests are additional automated testing practices discussed in this section.

The automated testing tools currently on the market are not always compatible with all environments or all testing needs. Some testing efforts may require custom test harnesses, either as a substitute for an off-the-shelf testing solution or to complement it. This section discusses when and why such tools should be developed, and the issues associated with them.

No single automation framework solution is best for all automation requirements. Automated test frameworks must be tailored to the organization's testing environment and to the task at hand. It is important that the appropriate automation test frameworks be chosen when developing an automated testing program.

Item 36: Do Not Rely Solely on Capture/Playback[1]

Functional testing tools (also called capture/playback tools) comprise just one of the numerous types of testing tools available. Capture/playback mechanisms can enhance the testing effort, but should not be the sole method used in automated testing. They have limitations, even when the best capture/playback automation techniques have been applied.

Capture/playback scripts must be modified after initial recording. Modification for functional testing focuses mostly on verifying tests through the GUI, also called **black-box** testing. To be most effective, black-box testing should be applied in combination with **gray-box** (internal-component based) and **white-box** (code-based) testing. Therefore, the most effective test automation involves additional automated testing tools and techniques beyond capture/playback.

Capture/playback is a feature of most automated test tools that enables the user to record keystrokes and mouse movements while interacting with an application. The keystrokes and mouse movements are recorded as a script, and can then be "played back" during test execution. While this method can be beneficial in specific situations, test scripts created using only capture/playback have significant limitations and drawbacks:

- *Hard-coded data values.* Capture/playback tools generate scripts based on user interactions including any data entered or received from the user interface.

---

1. Elfriede Dustin et al., "Reusable Test Procedures," Section 8.2.2 in *Automated Software Testing* (Reading, Mass: Addison-Wesley, 1999).

Having data values "hard coded" right in the script can create maintenance problems later. The hard-coded values may render the script invalid if the user interface or other aspects of the application change. For example, input values, window coordinates, window captions, and other values can be captured within the script code generated during recording. These fixed values can become problematic during test execution if any of these values has changed in the application: The test script may interact improperly with the application or fail altogether. Another problematic hard-coded value is the date stamp. When the test engineer captures the current date in a test procedure, and then activates the script on a later date, it will fail, because the hard-coded date value contained in the script no longer matches the current date.

- *Non-modular, hard-to-maintain scripts.* Capture/playback scripts generated by the testing tool are usually not modular, and as a result are hard to maintain. For example, a particular URL in a Web application may be referenced in a number of test procedures, so it follows that a single change to this URL can render a significant number of scripts unusable, if those scripts are using the hard-coded URL. A modular development approach references, or **wraps up**, the URL in only one function. That function is then called by the various scripts that use it, so any changes to the URL need to be made in only one place.

- *Lack of standards for reusability.* One of the most important issues in test-procedure development is reusability. A specific test-creation standard that addresses the development of reusable automated test procedures can vastly improve test-team efficiency. Encapsulating the user-interface portion of the tests into modular, reusable script files that can be called from other scripts can substantially reduce the effort of maintaining scripts for a constantly changing user interface.

  When creating a library of reusable functions, it is best to keep functionality such as data reading, writing, and validation, navigation, logic, and error checking separate, possibly in different script files. Automated-test development guidelines should be based on many of the same principles used for efficient software development. It is a good practice to follow the development-language guidelines that are closest to the development language of the scripts generated by the testing tool. For example, if the tool uses a C-like language, follow C development standards; if the tool uses a BASIC-like language, follow BASIC development standards.

It is evident that test scripts created exclusively using the capture/playback method for automated test development are difficult to maintain and reuse. In a few situations, basic scripts are useful; but in most cases, unless they modify the scripts after recording, test engineers would need to rerecord them many times during the test-execution process to account for any changes in the application under test. The potential advantages of using the capture/playback tool would thus be negated by the need to continually recreate the test scripts. This can lead to a high level of frustration among test personnel and general dissatisfaction with the automated testing tool.

To avoid the problems associated with unmodified capture/playback scripts, development guidelines for reusable test scripts should be created. Unmodified capture/playback scripting does not represent efficient test automation, and the exclusive use of capture/playback should be minimized.

Following these practices will improve the quality of capture/playback and automated testing. Still, it is important to realize that capture/playback tools, even when implemented using the best practices described in this chapter, are not the sole answer to test automation. Additional tools and techniques are required for effective testing to allow for more complete coverage and depth.

Item 37: Develop a Test Harness When Necessary

A *test harness* can be a tool that performs automated testing of the core components of a program or system. As used here, the term refers to code developed in-house that tests the underlying logic (back end) of an application. Off-the-shelf automated testing tools have their limitations, some of which are described in Item 32. Additionally, automation through the user interface is often too slow to be practical with thousands of test cases, and can be hampered by constant changes to the user interface.

To work around the limitations of an automated testing tool and allow deeper testing of core components, a test harness can be developed. Usually written in a robust programming language, as in a stand-alone C++ or VB program, a custom-built test harness typically is faster and more flexible than an automated test-tool script that may be constrained by the test tool's specific environment.

For an example of a testing task appropriate for a test harness, take an application whose purpose is to compute calculations based on user-supplied information and then generate reports based on those computations. The computations may be complex, and sensitive to different combinations of many possible input parameters. As a result, there could be millions of potential variations that produce different results, making comprehensive testing of the computations a significant undertaking.

It is very time-consuming to develop and verify thousands of computational test cases by hand. In most cases, it would be far too slow to execute a large volume of test cases through the user interface. A more effective alternative may be to develop a test harness that executes test cases against the application's code, typically below the user-interface layer, directly against core components.

Another way to use a test harness is to compare a new component against a legacy component or system. Often, two systems use different data-storage formats, and have different user interfaces with different technologies. In such a case, any automated test tool would require a special mechanism, or duplicate automated test scripts, in order to run identical test cases on the two systems and generate comparable results. In the worst case, a single testing tool is not compatible with both systems, so duplicate test scripts must be developed using two different automated testing tools. A better alternative would be to build a custom, automated test harness that encapsulates the differences between the two systems into separate modules and allows targeted testing to be performed against both systems. An automated test harness could take the test results generated by a legacy system as a baseline, and automatically verify the results generated by the new system by comparing the two result sets and outputting any differences.

One way to implement this is with a test harness adapter pattern. A **test-harness adapter** is a module that translates or "adapts" each system under test to make it compatible with the test harness, which executes pre-defined test cases against systems through the adapters, and stores the results in a standard format that can be automatically compared from one run to the next. For each system to be tested, a specific adapter must be developed that is capable of interacting with the system—directly against its DLLs or COM objects, for example—and executing the test cases against it. Testing two systems with a test harness would require two different test adapters and two separate invocations of the test harness, one for each system. The first invocation would produce a test result that would be saved and then compared against the test result for the second invocation. Figure 37.1 depicts a test harness capable of executing test cases against both a legacy system and a new system.

Identical test cases can be run against multiple systems using a test harness adapter for each system. The adapter for a legacy system can be used to establish a set of baseline results against which the results for the new system can be compared.

The test-harness adapter works by taking a set of test cases and executing them in sequence directly against the application logic of each system under test, bypassing the user interface. Bypassing the user interface optimizes performance, allowing for maximum throughput of the test cases. It also provides greater stability. If the test harness relied upon the user interface, any change to the interface (which often undergoes extensive revision during the development life cycle) could cause the test harness to report false positives. Reviewing such results would waste precious time.

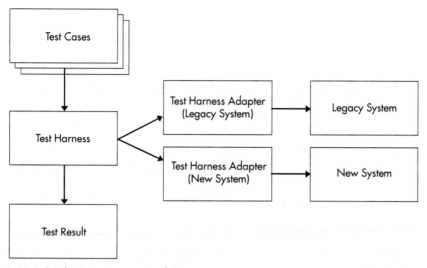

Figure 37.1. Basic Test-Harness Architecture

Results from each test case are stored in one or more results files, in a format (such as XML) that is the same regardless of the system under test. Results files can be retained for later comparison to results generated in subsequent test runs. The comparisons can be performed by a custom-built result-comparison tool programmed to read and evaluate the results files and output any errors or differences found. It is also possible to format the results so they can be compared with a standard "file diff" (file-difference comparison) tool.

As with any type of testing, test harness test cases may be quite complex, especially if the component tested by the harness is of a mathematical or scientific nature. Because there are sometimes millions of possible combinations of the various parameters involved in calculations, there are also potentially millions of possible test cases. Given time and budget constraints, it is unlikely that all possible cases will be tested; however, many thousands of test cases can feasibly be executed using a test harness.

With thousands of different test cases to be created and executed, test-case management becomes a significant effort. Detailed below is a general strategy for developing and managing test cases for use with a test harness. This strategy is also applicable to other parts of the testing effort.

1. *Create test cases.* Test cases for a test harness are developed in the same fashion as for manual testing, using various **test techniques**. A test technique is a

formalized approach to choosing test conditions that give a high probability of finding defects. Instead of guessing at which test cases to choose, test techniques help testers derive test conditions in a rigorous and systematic way. A number of books on testing describe testing techniques such as equivalence partitioning, boundary-value analysis, cause-effect graphing, and others. These are discussed in detail in Item 25, but a brief overview is provided here:

- **Equivalence partitioning** identifies the ranges of inputs and initial conditions expected to produce the same results. Equivalence relies on the commonality and variances among the different situations in which a system is expected to work.

- **Boundary-value testing** is used mostly for testing input-edit logic. Boundary conditions should always be part of the test scenarios, because many defects occur on the boundaries. Boundaries define three sets or classes of data: good, bad, and on-the-border (in-bound, out-of-bound, and on-bound).

- **Cause-effect graphing** provides concise representations of logical conditions and corresponding actions, shown in graph form with causes on the left and effects on the right.

- **Orthogonal-array testing** enables the selection of the combinations of test parameters that provide maximum coverage using a minimum number of test cases. Orthogonal-array test cases can be generated in an automated fashion.

2. *Establish a common starting point.* All testing must begin at a well-defined starting point that is the same every time the test harness is executed. Usually, this means the data used in each system during each test must be the same so that the results can be properly compared. When each modular test component is reused, it will be able to set the application state back to the way it found it for the next test component to run. Were this not the case, the second test component would always fail, because the assumed starting point would be incorrect.

3. *Manage test results.* Test scripts produce results for every transaction set they execute. These results are generally written to a file. A single test script can write results to as many files as desired, though in most cases a single file should be sufficient. When running a series of test cases, several test-results

files are created. Once baselined, any given test case should produce the same results every time it is executed, test-results files can be compared directly via simple file-comparison routines or by using a custom-developed test-results comparison tool. Any differences found during comparisons must be evaluated in order to identify, document, and track to closure the defects causing those differences.

A custom-built test harness can provide a level of testing above and beyond that of automated test-tool scripts. Although creating a test harness can be time-consuming, it offers various advantages, including deeper coverage of sensitive application areas and ability to compare two applications that cannot be tested using a single off-the-shelf test tool.

Item 38: Use Proven Test-Script Development Techniques

T est-script development can be regarded as a software development project of its own. Proven techniques should be used to produce efficient, maintainable, and reusable test scripts. This will require some additional work on the part of the test team, but in the end the testing effort will profit from a more effective automated testing product.

Consider the following techniques when developing test scripts using functional testing tools.

- *Data-driven framework.* **Data driven** means that data values are read from either spreadsheets or tool-provided data pools, rather than being hard coded into the test-procedure script. As mentioned in Item 37, capture/playback tools create scripts that contain hard-coded values. Generally it is recommended that the test engineer edit these scripts, because hard-coded data values often prevent test procedures from being reused. Hard-coded values should be replaced with variables, and whenever possible read data from external sources, such as an ASCII text file, a spreadsheet, or a database.

  The test team identifies the data scenarios, data elements, data value names, or data variable names to be used by the various test procedures. The key pieces of data added after a test-procedure script has been created via capture/playback are variable definitions and definitions of data sources (names and locations of files, spreadsheets, databases, and so on) from which the data values are to be read.

Externalizing input data also reduces data maintenance and increases flexibility. Whenever there is a need to execute a test procedure with a different set of data, the data source can be updated or changed as necessary.

- *Modular script development.* A common-software development technique used to increase maintainability and readability.of source code is to divide the code into logical **modules**, each of which performs a separate part of the job. These modules can then be called from multiple points in a script, so their code does not have to be rewritten each time, or modified in each script. This is especially important when a change is made to one of the modules—the change needs to be made in only one location, which reduces maintenance costs.

- *Modular user-interface navigation.* An especially important function of test scripts that should be modularized is the navigation of the application's user interface. To increase the reusability of test scripts, a test engineer should have the script use a navigation method that is least likely to be affected by changes in the application's user interface. Navigation functions should be kept in a separate module within the test library. The test requirement should specify whether test procedures developed using a test-tool recorder navigate through the application through the use of tabs, keyboard accelerator keys (hot keys), or mouse clicks, and whether they capture the x-y coordinates (not recommended) or the object names of particular objects, such as window names or names of HTML objects on a Web page.

All of these choices will potentially be affected by design changes to the application. For example, if test-procedure scripts are developed using tab-key navigation to move between objects, the resulting test scripts are tab-order dependent. If the tab order changes, all of the scripts potentially must be corrected, which can be a monumental task. If accelerator keys are used in the script, but subsequently changed in the application, the scripts must likewise be changed or replaced. Mouse playback can be disrupted if a user-interface control is moved, or is replaced by a different type of control.

Introducing a new type of control affects almost all scripts negatively—no matter what navigation method is used.[1] Modularizing the interaction

---

1. However, tools are becoming "smarter." For example, take Rational Software's RobotJ (see http://www.rational.com/products/tstudio/robotj.jsp, retrieved Sept. 8, 2002). Rational's new technology uses pattern matching. To validate changing data in interactive applications, the tester can set a range of acceptable data and replay tests with fewer problems than would occur with less sophisticated software tools.

with the control can help. Another way to avoid the problem is to navigate through an application by identifying fields by their object names or other unique identifiers assigned by the particular development tool. That way, a field can be moved to any position on the screen and the script will not be affected, because it navigates to the field by its name, not position. In this way, a recorded script can be made less susceptible to code changes and more reusable.

Similarly, whenever possible, the test procedure should make use of a window's object name, which is most likely to remain static, instead of identifying the window by caption. Depending on how scripts are designed, window or object information can be maintained in a spreadsheet. Navigation can be executed by using a driver that retrieves the various navigation information pieces from this spreadsheet. Some tools keep object information in a special GUI Map or Frame File. In such a case, it's not necessary to also put the information into a spreadsheet.

- *Libraries of reusable functions.* Test scripts typically perform many similar actions when acting upon the same product, and even with different products of the same type, such as Web applications. Separating these common actions into shared script libraries usable by all test engineers in the organization can greatly enhance the efficiency of the testing effort.

- *Pre-built libraries.* Pre-built libraries of functions for certain testing tools are available on the Internet. For example, a group of test engineers using the Win-Runner test tool created a library of reusable scripts and made them available to all test engineers via the Web.[2] The library contains templates for test scripts, extensions of the test-script languages, and standardized test procedures for GUI testing using WinRunner, a test tool from Mercury Interactive. Table 38.1 provides examples of reusable functions available for WinRunner.

  The library contains three basic sections: script templates, functions, and GUI checks. All three are designed to simplify the work of the test developer and to standardize the test results. The script templates provide

2. Tilo Linz and Matthias Daigl, "How to Automate Testing of Graphical User Interfaces" (Möhrendorf, Germany: imbus GmbH, n.d., retrieved Sept. 5, 2002 from http://www.imbus.de/engl/forschung/pie24306/gui/aquis-full_paper-1.3.html [text] and http://www.imbus.de/engl/forschung/pie24306/gui/gui_folien.html [accompanying slides]).

frameworks for test engineers writing their own scripts. The script functions can be copied, then developed into complete test scripts or function sets. GUI checks are integrated into the WinRunner environment by starting the corresponding installation script; they can then be used just like the GUI checks built into WinRunner.

Table 38.1. Reusable Functions of WinRunner Scripts

Module	Description
Array	Functions for associative arrays
File	Functions for file access
General	Miscellaneous universal functions
Geo	Functions for checking the geometric alignment of objects
List	Functions for simplified access to list objects
Menu	Functions for handling menus
Standard	Standard tests
StdClass	Standard tests for object classes, such as radio buttons
String	Functions for handling character strings
Tab	Functions for accessing tab-card controls
Tooltips	Functions for accessing tool tips and toolbars

- *Version control.* Although not a script-*development* technique per se, version control is a vital part of any software project. All test scripts should be stored in a version-control tool, such as Microsoft Visual SourceSafe, to ensure that they are protected from simultaneous changes by different test engineers, and that a history of changes to each file is maintained. Without a version-control tool, it is all too easy for different script developers to change the same file, putting the developers in the error-prone position of needing to manually merge their changes. In addition, tracking which scripts work with which software builds is much easier when using a version-control tool, because sets of scripts can be labeled into groups that can be retrieved at any time in the future.

Item 39: Automate Regression Tests When Feasible

R egression testing determines whether any errors were introduced into previously working functionality while fixing an earlier error or adding new functionality to an application. Providing valued customers with lots of new and
exciting features is of no benefit if the upgrade process manages to also break features they have been using successfully for the last several years. Regression testing
should catch these newly introduced defects. However, despite its recognized importance, regression testing remains the testing phase often given the least attention in
the planning of test activities.

An unplanned and manual approach can lead to inefficient and inadequate
regression testing and is an inefficient use of resources. In developing a well-planned,
effective regression test program, a number of questions must be answered:

- *When should regression tests be performed?* Regression testing is conducted for
  each change that may affect the functioning of previously baselined software.
  It includes all other previously run test procedures. Regression tests are also
  conducted when previously defective software that was corrected.

- *What should be included in the regression test?* Initially, regression testing
  should focus on high-risk functionality, and most-often executed paths.
  After these elements are tested, the more detailed functionality may be examined. Regression testing can entail a specific selection of automated tests that
  exercise high-risk and areas of code that are potentially affected by repair of
  defects, or it can involve rerunning an entire suite of tests.

In the ideal test environment, all necessary test procedures eventually are automated as part of the regression test suite as new features become available for testing (see below).

▪ *How can the regression test suite be optimized and improved?* A test engineer can optimize a regression test suite by performing the following steps.

1. Run the regression test set.

2. If cases are discovered for which the regression test set ran correctly but errors surfaced later, include the test procedures that identified those bugs and other related scenarios in the regression test set. (Defects can be uncovered after the regression testing phase, for example during further system testing or beta testing, or through tech support calls).

3. Repeat these steps, continually optimizing the regression test suite of scripts using quality measurements. (In this case, the relevant metric would be the number and types of test-procedure errors.)

In addition to following these steps, developers should provide information about the application areas directly affected by the implementation of new features and bug fixes and by other code changes. The information provided by the developers should be documented in a regression impacts matrix. Testers can use such a matrix to evaluate the regression test suite, determining whether the planned tests provide adequate coverage of the affected areas, and adding or modifying test procedures accordingly.

The regression impact matrix should allow for coverage of other areas in addition to the section of software that has been changed. Errors may appear where they are least expected. In the classic example of a regression error, one module is changed, so it is tested during system test; but the change made in this module also affects another module that uses the data created by the changed module. If regression tests cover only the directly changed areas, many regression issues are missed.

One important point to remember is that in the iterative and incremental development model, regression tests are also developed incrementally and must build on one another. Additionally, some regression tests must be changed or removed as parts of the applications change. Regression tests cannot be static: Modification of regression tests is necessary.

As discussed in Item 22, the basic set of test procedures is based on requirements. Therefore, there must be a process to ensure that any requirement changes are directly communicated to the testing team. Modifications to existing specifications require corresponding modifications of the regression test procedures to account for the application's new functionality. The testing team must have a direct line of communication to the requirements team. No changes to the requirements should take place without the testing team's awareness and sign-off.

Regression test cases should be traceable to the original requirement. This way, when requirements are changed or removed, the related test cases that need updating will be known. Regression test phases are typically conducted by simply rerunning existing test suites, hoping these will catch all problems. However, it is important that new test cases be added as the system under test evolves, to provide depth and coverage that encompasses the software in its amended state.

- *Why automate regression tests?* When dealing with a large, complex system, it is possible to end up with thousands upon thousands of regression tests, as feature test suites from previous releases are added to the regression program for the next release. It is necessary, therefore, that regression test suites be automated, and then executed in a stable test environment that allows running all of the tests quickly without using a lot of resources. If those tests were not automated, regression testing could turn the testing effort into a long, tedious process. Worse, some regression tests might never be executed, leaving big gaps in the testing effort.

  Additionally, manual execution of regression tests can be tedious, error prone, and lacking in coverage. Often, a test engineer feels that because a test was executed on a previous build or a fix was put in place in another area of the software, not the area currently under scrutiny, it is safe not to repeat that test. Other times, the production schedule might not allow for running an entire suite of manual regression tests. Because it is usually lengthy and tedious, and therefore prone to human error, regression testing should be done through an automated tool, a test harness, or a combination of the two.

  Some tools allow groups of test procedures to be created. For example, in Robot a **test shell** groups several test procedures and plays them back in a specific, predefined sequence. Executing a test shell or **wrapper** containing a complete set of system test scripts is an efficient use of automated scripts during regression testing. Such a procedure allows the test engineer to create and execute a comprehensive test suite, and then store the results of the test in a single output log.

It is in the area of regression testing that automated test tools provide the largest return on investment. All of the scripts that have been developed previously can be executed in succession to verify that no new errors are introduced when changes are made to fix defects. Because the scripts can be run with no manual intervention, they can easily be run as many times as necessary to detect errors. Automated testing allows for simple repeatability of tests.

A significant amount of testing is conducted on the basic user-interface operations of an application. When the application is sufficiently operable, test engineers can proceed to test business logic in the application and behavior in other areas. Portions of the regression suite can be used to make a simple **smoke test**—a condensed version of a regression test suite, as described in Item 40. With both manual and automated regression testing, the test teams repeatedly perform the same basic operability tests. For example, with each new release, the test team would verify that everything that previously worked still does.

Besides delaying the focus on other tests, the tedium of running regression tests manually exacts a very high toll on the testers. Manual testing can become delayed by the repetition of these tests, at the expense of progress on other required tests. Automated testing presents the opportunity to move more quickly and to perform more comprehensive testing within a given schedule. Automated regression testing frees up test resources, allowing test teams to turn their creativity and effort to more advanced test problems and concerns.

Automating regression testing also allows for after-hours testing, since most automated test tools provide the option for scripts to be executed at preset times without any user interaction. The test engineer can set up a test-script program in the morning, for example, to be executed by the automated test tool at 11 p.m. that night. The next day, the team can review the test-script output log and analyze the results.

- *How does one analyze the results of a regression test?* When errors are observed for a system functionality that previously worked, the test team must identify other functional areas most likely to have an effect on the function in which the error occurred. Based upon the results of such analysis, greater emphasis can be placed on regression testing for the affected areas. Once fixes have been implemented, regression testing is again performed on the problem area, to verify closure of the open defects and that no new defects have been introduced.

The test team must also identify particular components or functions that produce a relatively greater number of problem reports. As a result of this analysis, additional test procedures and effort may need to be assigned to those components. If developers indicate that a particular functional area is now *fixed*, yet regression testing continues to uncover problems for the software, the test engineer must ascertain whether an environment issue is at play, or poor implementation of the software correction is at fault.

Test results can also be analyzed to determine whether particular test procedures are worthwhile in terms of identifying errors. If a regression test case has not caught any errors yet, there is no guarantee it will not catch an error at the 50th regression run. However, it is important to evaluate the effectiveness and validity of each test as new and changed functionality is introduced. Test-results analysis is also another way to identify the functions where the most defects have been uncovered, and therefore where further test and repair efforts should be concentrated.

The preceding points can help the testing team create an effective regression test program. As with all testing techniques and approaches, it is important to make sure that automated regression testing makes sense for the project at hand. If the system is constantly changing, for example, the benefit of automating regression testing can be low for the extensive maintenance cost of keeping the automated tests current for the ever-evolving system. Therefore, before automating a regression test suite, it is important to determine that the system is stable, that its functionality, underlying technology, and implementation are not constantly changing.

Item 40: Implement Automated Builds and Smoke Tests

Automated builds are typically executed once or twice per day (perhaps overnight), using the latest set of stable code. Developers can pull the components from the build machine each day, or rebuild locally themselves if they so desire.

A **smoke test** is a condensed version of a regression test suite. It is focused on automated testing of the critical high-level functionality of the application. Instead of having to repeatedly retest everything manually whenever a new software build is received, the smoke test is played against the software, verifying that the major functionality still operates properly.

Using an automated test tool, the test engineer records the test steps that would otherwise be manually performed in software-build verification. Typically, this verification is performed after the system is compiled, unit tested, and integration tested. It should be regarded as the "entrance criterion" for starting the testing phase for that build.

Implementing automated builds can greatly streamline the efforts of the development and configuration-management teams. Large software systems are typically built after-hours, so that a new build can be ready for the next day.[1] Any problems

---

1. On large projects, sophisticated configuration-management or **process-management** tools are usually required to perform frequent builds. So-called **enterprise-level** tools go far beyond the simple file-based version control of simpler, less-costly tools. They allow a working version of the software to be built at almost any time, even when several developers are making widespread changes.

encountered by the build process during its unattended operation must be resolved as soon as possible, however, so that development progress is not delayed. Some organizations use automated notification technologies that send emails or text pages to contact the appropriate personnel if a software build or regression test fails. Depending on the length of the build or regression test, this can be critical, allowing the problem to be corrected prior to the start of the next business day.

In addition to automating the software build, an automated smoke test can further optimize the development and testing environments. Software is always ready to use after the build, in a known good condition, because the smoke test will have automatically verified the build. If the unit-testing practices outlined in Chapter 6 are also part of the build process, the development and testing teams can be confident that the number of defects in the build has been significantly reduced by the time the software is ready to be tested.

If all of the aforementioned practices are followed, the typical software build sequence is as follows:

1. Software build (compilation), possibly including unit tests as described in Chapter 6

2. Smoke test

3. Regression test

If an error occurs at any point in the process, the entire cycle halts. After the problem is corrected, the build sequence is restarted at the appropriate point.

To build a smoke test, the test team first determines which parts of the application make up the high-level functionality, and then develops automated procedures for testing the major parts of the system. In this context, **major** refers to the basic operations that are used most frequently and can be exercised to determine if there are any large flaws in the software. Examples of major functions include logging on, adding records, deleting records, and generating reports.

Smoke tests may also comprise a series of tests verifying that the database points to the correct environment, the database is the correct version, sessions can be launched, all screens and menu selections are accessible, and data can be entered, selected and edited. When testing the first release of an application, the test team may wish to perform a smoke test on each available part of the system in order to begin test development as soon as possible without having to wait for the entire system to stabilize.

If the results meet expectations, meaning that the application under test has passed the smoke test, the software is formally moved into the test environment. Otherwise, the build should not be considered ready for testing.

CHAPTER 9
Nonfunctional Testing[1]

The nonfunctional aspects of an application or system, such as performance, security, compatibility, and usability, can require considerable effort to test and perfect. Meeting nonfunctional requirements can make the difference between an application that merely performs its functions, and one that is well received by its end-users and technical support personnel, and is readily maintainable by system administrators.

It is a mistake to ignore nonfunctional system requirements until late in the application's development life cycle. The potential impact on the system architecture and implementation, which may need to change in order to satisfy these needs, necessitates consideration of nonfunctional requirements early in the development life cycle. Ideally, nonfunctional requirements are treated as important characteristics of the application. Therefore, proper documentation of nonfunctional aspects in the requirements can be vital to the development of a well-received application.

In Chapter 1, it is recommended that nonfunctional requirements are associated with their corresponding functional requirements and defined during the requirements phase. If nonfunctional requirements are not defined, the requirements as a whole should be considered incomplete; unless defined early on, these important aspects of the system will probably not receive the appropriate attention until late in the development life cycle.

---

1. Nonfunctional requirements do not endow the system with additional functions, but rather constrain or further define how the system will perform any given function.

Item 41: Do Not Make Nonfunctional Testing an Afterthought[1]

Typically, the requirements, development, and testing efforts of a software project are so focused on the functionality of the system that the nonfunctional aspects of the software are overlooked until the very end. Certainly, if an application or system does not have the appropriate functionality, then it cannot be considered a success. The argument may also be made that nonfunctional issues can be addressed at a later time, such as with a version upgrade or patch.

Unfortunately, this approach can lead to problems in the application's implementation, and even increased risk of failure in production. For example, ignoring security on a Web application for the sake of implementing functionality may leave it vulnerable to attack from malicious Internet users, which in turn can result in downtime, loss of customer data, and negative public attention to the site, ultimately resulting in loss of revenue. As another example, consider an application that is functionally complete, but unable to process a sufficient amount of customer data. Although the application provides the proper functions, it is useless because it does not meet the customer's needs. Again, problems like these can lead to negative publicity for the application and lost customers. These kinds of problems can often undo the effort spent to implement functionality, and can take an enormous amount of effort to correct.

---

1. For detailed discussion of nonfunctional implementation, see Elfriede Dustin et al., *Quality Web Systems* (Boston, Mass.: Addison-Wesley, 2002).

Nonfunctional considerations ideally are investigated early in an application's architecture and design phases. Without early attention to these aspects of the implementation, it may be difficult or impossible later to modify or add components to satisfy the nonfunctional requirements. Consider the following examples:

- *Web-application performance.* Web applications are typically developed in small environments, such as one consisting of a single Web server and a single database server. In addition, when the system is first placed into production, it is most cost effective to use the minimum hardware necessary to service the initially small number of users. Over time, however, the load on the Web application may increase, requiring a corresponding increase in the site's hardware capacity to handle the load. If the hardware capacity is not increased, users will experience performance problems, such as excessive time for loading pages and possibly even time-outs at the end-user's browser. Typically, Web-site capacity is increased by adding several machines to the site to **scale** the Web application to achieve higher performance. If this type of expansion was not considered in the application's original architecture and implementation, considerable design and implementation changes may be required to achieve scalability. This results in higher costs, and, perhaps worst of all, considerable delay as engineers work to develop and roll out the improved production site.

- *Use of an incompatible third-party control.* One way to increase an application's functionality while reducing development time is to use third-party controls, such as ActiveX controls, for parts of the user interface. However, these controls may not be compatible with all platforms or installations. If an application is released without verifying the compatibility of its components with all user environments and an incompatibility is later identified, there may be no choice but to remove the third-party control and provide an alternate or custom implementation, requiring extra development and testing time. Meanwhile, the organization is unable to serve some users until the new version of the application is ready.

- *Concurrency in a multiuser client-server application.* Multiuser access to an application is one of the primary features of the client-server architecture. In client-server systems, concurrency, or simultaneous access to application data, is a major concern because unexpected behavior can occur if, for example, two users attempt to modify the same item of data. A strategy for handling data isolation is necessary to ensure that the data remains consistent in a multiuser environment. This strategy is typically implemented in the lower levels of the application, or in some cases in the user interface. If concurrency issues are not considered in the architecture and design of the application, components must later be modified to accommodate this requirement.

The risks of ignoring the nonfunctional aspects of an application until late in the development cycle must be considered by any organization, regardless of the type of software product being developed. Although it may be decided that some risks cannot be addressed immediately, it is better to know and plan for them than to be surprised when problems surface.

When planning a software project, consider the following nonfunctional risks:

- *Poor performance.* Poor application performance may be merely an inconvenience, or it may render the application worthless to the end user. When evaluating the performance risk of an application, consider the need for the application to handle large quantities of users and data. (Item 42 discusses large data sets.) In server-based systems, such as Web applications, failure to evaluate performance can leave scaling capabilities unknown, and lead to inaccurate cost estimates, or lack of cost estimates, for system growth.

- *Incompatibility.* The proper functioning of an application on multiple end-user system configurations is of primary concern in most software-development activities. Incompatibilities can result in many technical-support calls and product returns. As with poor performance, compatibility problems may be mere nuisances, or they may prevent the application from functioning at all.

- *Inadequate security.* Although security should be considered for all applications, Web-based software projects must be particularly concerned with this aspect. Improper attention to security can result in compromised customer data, and can even lead to legal action. If the application is responsible for sensitive customer information, security lapses can cause a severe loss of reputation, and possibly legal action.

- *Insufficient usability.* Inadequate attention to the usability aspects of an application can lead to a poor acceptance rate among end users, based on the perception that the application is difficult to use, or that it doesn't perform the necessary functions. This can trigger an increase in technical support calls, and can negatively affect user acceptance and application sales.

To avert such problems, it is very important to assess the nonfunctional aspects of an application as early as possible in the development life cycle.

It is equally important, however, not to overcompensate with too much attention to nonfunctional concerns. When addressing nonfunctional areas, there are typically tradeoffs. For example, consider application performance: Some software projects place so much emphasis on having well-performing applications that they underemphasize good design—two concepts that are often at odds. This can lead to code that is difficult to maintain or expand at a later point. Security provides another example of trade-offs: Architecting an application for maximum security can lead to poor application performance. It is critical that the risks of focusing on such nonfunctional issues as security or performance be weighed against the corresponding sacrifices to other aspects of the application.

It is most beneficial to the testing team if the nonfunctional requirements of an application are considered along with the functional aspects during the requirements phase of development. Requirements documents can specify performance or security constraints for each user interaction. This makes it possible not only for developers to ensure that the nonfunctional requirements are satisfied in the application's implementation, but also for the testing team to devise test cases for these concerns. Test procedures should include areas for each nonfunctional test for a given requirement, as described in Item 21.

In addition to specific requirements-level nonfunctional information, it is also useful to have a set of **global** nonfunctional constraints that apply to all requirements. This eliminates the need to repeatedly state the same nonfunctional concerns in every requirements document.

Nonfunctional requirements are usually documented in two ways:

1. A system-wide specification is created that defines nonfunctional requirements for all use cases in the system. An example: "The user interface of the Web system must be compatible with Netscape Navigator 4.x or higher and Microsoft Internet Explorer 4.x or higher."

2. Each requirement description contains a section titled "Nonfunctional Requirements," which documents any specific nonfunctional needs of that particular requirement that differ from the system-wide specifications.

Item 42: Conduct Performance Testing with Production-Sized Databases

Testing teams responsible for an application that manages data must be cognizant that application performance typically degrades as the amount of data stored by the application increases. Database and application optimization techniques can greatly reduce this degradation. It is critical, therefore, to test the application to ensure that optimization has been successfully employed.

To chart application performance across data sets of different sizes, it is usually necessary to test with a variety of data sets. For example, an application may be tested with 1, 100, 500, 1,000, 5,000, 10,000, 50,000, and 100,000 records to investigate how the performance changes as the data quantity grows. This type of testing also makes it possible to find the "upper bound" of the application's data capability, meaning the largest database with which the application performs acceptably.

It is critical to begin application performance testing as soon as possible in the development life cycle. This allows performance improvements to be incorporated while the application is still under development, rather than after significant portions of the application have been developed and tested. Early on, it is acceptable to focus on general performance testing, as opposed to performance fine-tuning. During the early stages, any glaring performance problems should be corrected; finer tuning and optimization issues can be addressed later in the development cycle.

Often, a generic set of sample data will be created early in the project, and—because of time constraints—that data will be used throughout much, if not all, of the development and functional testing. Unfortunately, data sets such as these tend to be unrealistic, with insufficient size and variation, which may result in performance surprises when an actual customer, using much more data than contained in the sample data set, attempts to use the application. For this reason, it is recommended that testing teams, and perhaps development teams, use production-sized databases that include a wide range of possible data combinations and scenarios while the application is under development. Although it will take some extra time up-front to create these databases, it is worth the effort to avoid a crisis when the application goes into production.

Working with databases of realistic size also has secondary benefits to the project. Large databases can be difficult to handle and maintain. For example, building a large data set may require significant disk space and processor power. Storing data sets of this size may require additional resources, such as large disk drives or tapes. Depending on the application, large data sets may also lead to backup and recoverability concerns. If data is transferred across a network, or the Internet, bandwidth may also be a consideration for both the application and any additional processing performed on the data by support personnel. Working with realistic data sets as early as possible will help bring these issues to the surface while there is time, and when it is more cost-effective, to do something about them, rather than after the application or system is already in a production environment, when such issues can become very costly to address in terms of both budget and schedule.

There are a few ways to determine and create the appropriate data for a large data set, many of which are discussed in Item 10. It is usually necessary to consult the development, product-management, and requirements teams to determine which parts of the data are the most critical, as well as which are most variable. For example, the database for an order-processing application may contain many tables full of information, but the most variable of these tables are those that store the details of orders and the customer information.

Once the necessary data elements are known, it may be possible to randomly generate (through a script or other program) a large number of records to increase the size of the database. Be aware, however, that randomly generated data may not be useful for *functional* testing, because it may not reflect real data scenarios that would be entered by a user. It is usually necessary to employ separate special-purpose data sets for functional testing and performance testing.

One way to gather realistic data is to poll potential or existing customers to learn about the data they use or plan to use in the application. This should be done during the requirements phase, while investigating how large the largest data set could be, what the average database size is, and so on. To use the previous example, it may be determined that the potential customers of the order-processing system have data sets that range from 1,000 to 100,000 orders. This information should be placed into the business case for the application, as well as the global nonfunctional requirements specifications. Once the decision is made to focus on supporting this range of order quantities, test databases can be created that reflect the smallest and largest anticipated sets of orders, as well as increments in between.

If the application being developed is a Web or client-server application, the production-class hardware that will ultimately run the software is typically more powerful than the hardware available for testing and development. A production-class machine will most likely have faster and multiple processors, faster disks, and more RAM. Due to cost constraints, most organizations will not provide production-class hardware for the development and testing environments.

This makes it necessary to extrapolate performance based on the differences between testing and production hardware platforms. Such estimations usually require baselining to determine a performance ratio between the platforms. Once an estimated performance multiple is determined, performance tests on the less-robust hardware can be used to verify the application's ability to handle large data with a reasonable amount of confidence. It should be kept in mind, however, that extrapolations are only rough estimates, since many factors can cause performance differences between two systems.

Item 43: Tailor Usability Tests to the Intended Audience

Usability testing is a difficult, but necessary, step toward delivering an application that satisfies the needs of its users. The primary goal of usability testing is to verify that the intended users of the application are able to interact properly with the application while having a positive and convenient experience. This requires examination of the layout of the application's interface, including navigation paths, dialog controls, text, and other elements, such as localization and accessibility. Supporting components, such as the installation program, documentation, and help system, must also be investigated.

Proper development and testing of an application for usability requires understanding the target audience and its needs. This requirement should be prominently featured in the application's business case and other high-level documents.

There are several ways to determine the needs of the target audience from a usability perspective:

- *Subject-matter experts.* Having staff members who are also experts in the domain area is a necessity in the development of a complex application. It can be a great asset to have such staff members counseling the requirements, development, and testing teams on a continual basis. Most projects, in fact, require several subject-matter experts, as opinions on domain-related rules and processes can differ.

- *Focus groups.* An excellent way to get end-user input on a proposed user interface is to hold focus-group meetings to get potential customers' comments on what they would like to see in an interface. Prototypes and screenshots are useful tools in focus-group discussions. To ensure adequate coverage, it is important to select focus groups that are representative of all types of end users of the product.

- *Surveys.* Although not as effective as subject-matter experts and focus groups, surveys can yield valuable information about how potential customers would use a software product to accomplish their tasks.

- *Study of similar products.* Investigating similar products can provide information on how the problem has been solved by other groups, in the same and different problem domains. Although user interfaces should not be blatantly copied from other products, it is useful to study how other groups or competitors have chosen to approach the user interface.

- *Observation of users in action.* Monitoring a user's interaction with an application's interface can provide a wealth of information about its usability. This can be done by simply taking notes while a user works with the application, or by videotaping a session for later analysis. Observing users in action enables the usability tester to see where the users stumble with the user interface and where they find it intuitively easy.

As with most nonfunctional requirements, early attention to usability issues can produce much better results than attempting to retrofit the application at a later time. For example, some application designs and architectures may not be suitable for the required user interface; it would be exceptionally difficult to recover if it were determined late in the process that the application architecture could not support good usability. In addition, much time and effort goes into crafting the application's user interface, so it is wise to specify the correct interface as early as possible in the process.

An effective tool in the development of a usable application is the user-interface prototype. This kind of prototype allows interaction between potential users, requirements personnel, and developers to determine the best approach to the application's interface. Although this can be done on paper, prototypes are far superior because they are interactive and provide a more-realistic preview of what the application will look like. In conjunction with requirements documents, prototypes can also provide an early basis for developing test procedures, as described in Item 24. During the prototyping phase, usability changes can be implemented without much impact on the development schedule.

Later in the development cycle, end-user representatives or subject-matter experts should participate in usability tests. If the application is targeted at several types of end users, at least one representative from each group should take part in the tests. Participants can use the software at the site of the development organization, or a pre-release version can be sent to the end user's site along with usability-evaluation instructions. End-user testers should note areas where they don't find the interface understandable or usable, and should provide suggestions for improvement. Since, at this stage in the development life cycle, large-scale changes to the application's user interface are typically not practical, requests for feedback should be targeted toward smaller refinements.

A similar approach can be taken for an application that is already in production. Feedback and survey forms are useful tools in determining usability improvements for the next version of the application. Such feedback can be extremely valuable, coming from paying customers who have a vested interest in seeing the application improved to meet their needs.

Item 44: Consider All Aspects of Security, for Specific Requirements and System-Wide

Security requirements, like other nonfunctional issues, should be associated with each functional requirement. Each functional requirement likely has a specific set of related security issues to be addressed in the software implementation, in addition to security requirements that apply system-wide. For example, the log-on requirement in a client-server system must specify the number of retries allowed, the action to take if the log on fails, and so on. Other functional requirements have their own security-related requirements, such as maximum lengths for user-supplied inputs.[1]

With the security-related requirements properly documented, test procedures can be created to verify that the system meets them. Some security requirements can be verified through the application's user interface, as in the case of input-length checking. In other cases, it may be necessary to use gray-box testing, as described in Item 16, to verify that the system meets the specified requirement. For example, the requirements for the log-on feature may specify that user name and password must be transmitted in encrypted form. A network-monitoring program must be used to examine the data packets sent between the client and the server to verify that the

---

1. Input-length checking is vital for preventing buffer-overflow attacks on an application. For more information, see Elfriede Dustin et al., *Quality Web Systems* (Boston, Mass.: Addison-Wesley, 2002), 76–79.

225

credentials are in fact encrypted. Still other requirements may require analysis of database tables or of files on the server's hard disk.

In addition to security concerns that are directly related to particular requirements, a software project has security issues that are global in nature, and therefore are related to the application's architecture and overall implementation. For example, a Web application may have a global requirement that all private customer data of any kind is stored in encrypted form in the database. Because this requirement will undoubtedly apply to many functional requirements throughout the system, it must be examined relative to each requirement. Another example of a system-wide security requirement is a requirement to use SSL (Secure Socket Layer) to encrypt data sent between the client browser and the Web server. The testing team must verify that SSL is correctly used in all such transmissions. These types of requirements are typically established in response to assessments of risk, as discussed in Item 41.

Many systems, particularly Web applications, make use of third-party resources to fulfill particular functional needs. For example, an e-commerce site may use a third-party payment-processing server. These products must be carefully evaluated to determine whether they are secure, and to ensure that they are not employed improperly, in ways that could result in security holes. It is particularly important for the testing team to verify that any information passed through these components adheres to the global security specifications for the system. For example, the testing team must verify that a third-party payment-processing server does not write confidential information to a log file that can be read by an intruder if the server is compromised.

It is important to also keep up with and install the latest vendor supplied patches for third-party products. This includes patches for Web servers, operating systems, and databases. Microsoft, for example, provides frequent security updates for its Internet Information Server (IIS) as security problems are found. Although it is usually not necessary to verify that the supplied security patches correct the advertised problem, it is important to have personnel monitoring the status of security patches for the third-party products used in the system. As with all updates, the system should be regression tested after the installation of any patch to verify that new problems have not been introduced.

If the security risk associated with an application has been determined to be substantial, it is worth investigating options for outsourcing security-related testing. E-commerce sites, online banking, and other sites that deal in sensitive customer data should regard security as a high priority, because a break-in could mean disaster for the site and the organization. There are many third-party security-testing firms that will investigate the site, and possibly its implementation, for security flaws using the latest tools and techniques. Outsourcing in combination with in-house testing of security-related nonfunctional requirements is an excellent way to deliver a secure application.

Item 45: Investigate the System's Implementation To Plan for Concurrency Tests

I n a multiuser system or application, **concurrency** is a major issue that the development team must address. Concurrency, in the context of a software application, is the handling of multiple users attempting to access the same data at the same time.

For example, consider a multiuser order processing system that allows users to add and edit orders for customers. Adding orders is not a problem—since each new order generates a discrete record, several users can simultaneously add orders to the database without interfering with one another.

Editing orders, on the other hand, can result in concurrency problems. When a user opens an order to edit it, a dialog is displayed on the local machine with information about that order. To accomplish this, the system retrieves the data from the database and stores it temporarily in the local machine's memory, so the user can see and change the data. Once changes are made, the data is sent back to the server, and the database record for that order is updated. Now, if two users simultaneously have the editing dialog open for the same record, they both have copies of the data in their local machines' memory, and can make changes to it. What happens if they both choose to save the data?

The answer depends on how the application is designed to deal with concurrency. Managing multiuser access to a shared resource is a challenge that dates back to the introduction of multiuser mainframes. Any resource that can be accessed by more than one user requires software logic to protect that resource by managing the way multiple users can access and change it at the same time. This problem has only become more common since the advent of network file sharing, relational data-bases, and client-server computing.

There are several ways for a software application to deal with concurrency. Among these are the following:

- *Pessimistic.* This concurrency model places **locks** on data. If one user has a record open and any other users attempt to read that data in a context that allows editing, the system denies the request. In the preceding example, the first user to open the order for editing gets the lock on the order record. Sub-sequent users attempting to open the order will be sent a message advising that the order is currently being edited by another user, and will have to wait until the first user saves the changes or cancels the operation. This concur-rency model is best in situations when it is highly likely that more than one user will attempt to edit the same data at the same time. The downside with this model is that others users are prevented from accessing data that any one user has open, which makes the system less convenient to use. There is also a certain amount of implementation complexity when a system must manage record locks.

- *Optimistic.* In the optimistic concurrency model, users are always allowed to read the data, and perhaps even to update it. When the user attempts to save the data, however, the system checks to see if the data has been updated by any-one else since the user first retrieved it. If it has been changed, the update fails. This approach allows more users to view data than does the pessimistic model, and is typically used when it is unlikely that several users will attempt to edit the same data at the same time. However, it is inconvenient when a user spends time updating a record only to find that it cannot be saved. The record must be retrieved anew and the changes made again.

- *No concurrency protection: "last one wins."* The simplest model of all, this approach does not attempt to protect users from editing the same data. If two users open a record and make changes, the second user's changes will overwrite the first's in a "last-one-wins" situation. The first user's changes will be lost. Also, depending on how the system is implemented, this approach could lead to data corruption if two users attempt to save at the same moment.

The way a software application deals with concurrency can affect the performance, usability, and data integrity of the system. Therefore, it is important to design tests to verify that the application properly handles concurrency, following the concurrency model that has been selected for the project.

Testing application concurrency can be difficult. To properly exercise the system's concurrency handling techniques, timing is an issue. Testers must simulate two attempts to read or write data at the same instant to properly determine whether the system properly guards the data, whether by the establishment of locks in the case of pessimistic locking, or by checking for an update prior to saving data, as in the case of optimistic locking.

A combination of manual and automated techniques can be used for concurrency testing. Two test engineers can attempt to access the data through the user interface on separate machines, coordinating verbally to ensure that they access the data simultaneously. Automation can be used to exercise the system with higher volume, and more-reliable instantaneous access, possibly below the user-interface layer, to uncover any concurrency related issues. Knowledge of the system's implementation is key to designing and executing the appropriate tests.

Concurrency testing becomes more complicated when the same data can be updated via different interfaces or functions in the system. For example, if one user is editing a record, and another user deletes the record, the system must enforce the appropriate concurrency control. If pessimistic locking is in place, the system should not allow the record to be deleted while it is being edited. In fact, all functions that could potentially access the record should be tested to ensure that they cannot modify it while it is being edited.

The system-wide nonfunctional specifications should spell out how the system is to handle concurrency issues in general. If there are any deviations for individual system functions, these should be noted in the requirement documentation for those particular functions. For example, the system-wide specification may call for optimistic concurrency, while one particularly sensitive area of the system requires pessimistic concurrency. That fact must be noted in the documentation for the requirements in that specific system area.

Test procedures necessarily vary depending upon the concurrency approach taken by the system, and, as described in the preceding example, within parts of the system. It is essential that the testing team understand the concurrency handling approaches used in the system, because it is difficult to implement appropriate tests without this knowledge. Each concurrency model has nuances that must be accounted for in the test procedures.

The following list details some test-procedure concerns for each of the different concurrency models:

- *Pessimistic.* Because the application forcibly restricts users from accessing data while that data is being edited, the main concern in testing a pessimistic concurrency scheme is to verify that locks on records are properly acquired, released, and enforced in all areas of the application that may attempt to update the record. There are three primary areas of concern here:

  - *Lock acquisition.* Because only one user at a time can enter an update state with a particular record or item of data, it is critical that the system properly assign the lock to the user who requests it first. Improper implementation of lock-acquisition code could lead multiple users to believe they have the lock, in which case they will probably encounter errors or unexpected behavior when they attempt to save the data. Lock acquisition can be tested by having two users attempt to enter an edit state at the same instant, or with heavy volume. For the latter, a script may be employed to generate, say, 1,000 or more simultaneous requests to edit data and verify that only one is allowed to proceed.

  - *Lock enforcement.* Once a user has a lock, the system must ensure that the data cannot be modified in any way, including updates and deletions, by any other user. This is typically accomplished by having one user hold a record open—enter edit mode and stay there—while other users attempt to edit, delete, or otherwise update the data in all areas of the application. The system should reject all other users' attempts at updating the data.

  - *Lock release.* Another tricky area within pessimistic concurrency is lock release. Testers must verify that the system successfully makes the record available to other users once it has been released by the editing user, whether that user has chosen to go through with the update or cancel it. An important aspect of lock release is error handling—what happens if the user who holds the lock encounters an error, such as a client system crash. Is the lock orphaned (left in place with no way to release it)? The ability of the system to recover from failure to release a lock is an important concern.

- *Optimistic.* The optimistic concurrency model is somewhat less complex to implement. Because all users are allowed to retrieve and edit the data, the point of update is the only concern. As mentioned previously, a combination of manual and automated techniques offers the best approach to testing optimistic concurrency. In the manual approach, two testers edit the data and then attempt to save it at precisely the same time. The first user should get a successful update, while the second is sent a message that another user has updated the record, and to reload the record and make the changes again.

  In addition to manual testing, an automated, volume-oriented approach should be used. Using a script that attempts hundreds or thousands of updates at the same instant can ensure that the optimistic locking mechanism allows only one user at a time to update the record. The rest should receive error messages indicating that the record cannot be saved because another user has updated it.

  As with pessimistic concurrency, testers must verify that optimistic concurrency is enforced everywhere the data can be modified, including any possibilities for modification through different areas of the user interface.

- *No concurrency control.* The most basic, and error-prone, approach is a system with no concurrency control. Testing such a system is similar to testing optimistic concurrency, with the exception that all users should achieve successful updates regardless of the order in which they request the updates. Again, a combination of manual and automated testing techniques should be used, but with an emphasis on data integrity, an area for concern when there is no concurrency control. Testers should also ensure that update errors, such as when a record is deleted while another user is attempting to update it, are properly handled.

Investigating the system's implementation plan will help the test team determine the correct type of concurrency testing to perform. Because concurrency is a common problem area in most multiuser systems, proper testing of this area is essential.

Item 46: Set Up an Efficient Environment for Compatibility Testing

T esting an application for compatibility can be a complex job. With so many different operating system, hardware, and software configurations available, the number of possible combinations can be high. Unfortunately, there really isn't any way around the compatibility test problem—software either runs properly on any given system or it doesn't. An appropriate environment for compatibility testing can, however, make this process more efficient.

The business case for the system being developed should state all of the targeted end-user operating systems (and server operating systems, if applicable) on which the application must run. Other compatibility requirements must be stated as well. For example, the product under test may need to operate with certain versions of Web browsers, with hardware devices such as printers, or with other software, such as virus scanners or word processors.

Compatibility may also extend to upgrades from previous versions of the software. Not only must the system itself properly upgrade from a previous version, but the data and other information from the previous version must be considered as well. Is it necessary for the application to be backward compatible with data produced by a previous version? Should the user's preferences and other settings be retained after the upgrade? These questions and others must be answered in comprehensively assessing the compatibility situation.

With all the possible configurations and potential compatibility concerns, it probably is impossible to explicitly test every permutation. Software testers should consider ranking the possible configurations in order, from most to least common for the target application. For example, if most users run Windows 2000 with MS Internet Explorer 6.0 on dial-up connections, then that configuration should be at the top of list, and must be emphasized in the compatibility tests. For some of the less-common configurations, time and cost constraints may limit the testing to quick smoke tests.

In addition to selecting the most-important configurations, testers must identify the appropriate test cases and data for compatibility testing. Unless the application is small, it is usually not feasible to run the entire set of possible test cases on every possible configuration, because this would take too much time. Therefore, it is necessary to select the most representative set of test cases that confirms the application's proper functioning on a particular platform. In addition, testers also need appropriate test data to support those test cases. If performance is a compatibility concern for the application—for example, if it works with an open-ended amount of data—then testers will also need data sets of sufficient size.

It is important to continually update the compatibility test cases and data as issues are discovered with the application—not only while it is in development, but also once it is released. Tech-support calls can be a good source of information when selecting tests to add to the compatibility test suite. The calls may also provide an indication whether the most appropriate configurations were selected for compatibility testing, possibly leading to a revised set of configurations with different priority rankings.

A beta-test program is another potential source of information on end-user configurations and compatibility issues. A widely distributed beta test can provide a large set of data regarding real end-user configurations and compatibility issues prior to the final release of the application.

Managing the compatibility test environment can be a major undertaking. To properly test the application, it is best to precisely recreate the end-user environment. This is accomplished by installing actual operating system, hardware, and software configurations and executing the selected set of test procedures on each installation. As discussed previously, however, users may have many combinations of configurations. It is usually not cost effective to purchase and install all the machines needed to represent every potential test configuration; moreover, reinstalling even one or a few machines from the ground up for each new test is very costly. Therefore, a different approach must be taken.

A practical and cost-effective approach involves the use of removable hard drives in combination with a partition-management tool. This allows a small number of machines to potentially run a large number of configurations. The tester simply places the correct drive in the bay, reboots, and selects the desired configuration. There are many partition management tools on the market that can be used in this context, such as Partition Magic.

An alternative approach would be to use a drive-imaging program, such as Symantec Ghost, to create image files of the necessary configurations. These images can be used later to recreate the configuration on a target machine. The downside with this approach is that it can take a significant amount of time to recreate the configuration from the image, depending on the size of the installation. In addition, the image files can be quite large, so a way of managing them must be established.

Regardless of the technique used to manage the installations, once the proper configuration environment has been booted on the target machine, configuration tests can then be executed and analyzed to determine the application's compatibility on that platform.

In compatibility testing, the manner in which the application is installed on the target configuration is important. It is critical that the application be installed in the exact way the end user will install it, using the same versions of the components and the same installation procedures. This is best accomplished when an installation program is made available early in the development effort, and the software is provided to the testing team in an installable form, rather than a specialized package created by the development team. If a specialized or manual method of installation is used, the test environment may not mirror the end user's environment, and compatibility-test results may be inaccurate. It is also critical that no development tools be installed on the compatibility-test platform, because they may "taint" the environment so that it is not an exact reflection of the real operating conditions.

CHAPTER 10

Managing Test Execution

T est execution is the phase that follows after everything discussed to this point. With test strategies, test planning, test procedures designed and developed, and the test environment operational, it is time to execute the tests created in the preceding phases.

Once development of the system is underway and software builds become ready for testing, the testing team must have a precisely defined workflow for executing tests, tracking defects found, and providing information, or metrics, on the progress of the testing effort.

The items that follow discuss the participation of many teams throughout the organization, including testing, development, product management, and others, in test execution. It is the job of all of these teams to ensure that defects are found, prioritized, and corrected.

Item 47: Clearly Define the Beginning and End of the Test-Execution Cycle

Regardless of the testing phase, it is important to define the **entrance criteria** (when testing can begin) and the **exit criteria** (when testing is complete) for a software test execution cycle.

The entrance criteria describe when a testing team is ready to start testing a specific build. In order to accept a software build during system testing, various criteria should be met. Some examples:

- All unit and integration tests have been executed successfully.

- The software builds (compiles) without any issues.

- The build passes a smoke test, as discussed in Item 40.

- The build has accompanying documentation (**release notes**) describing what's new in the build and what has been changed.

- Defects have been repaired and are ready for retesting. (See Item 49 for a discussion of the defect-tracking life cycle.)

- The source code is stored in a version-control system.

Only after the entrance (or acceptance) criteria have been met is the testing team ready to accept the software build and begin the testing cycle.

Just as it is important to define the entrance criteria for a testing phase, exit criteria must also be developed. Exit criteria describe when the software has been adequately tested. Like entrance criteria, they depend on the testing phase. Because testing resources are finite, the test budget and number of test engineers are limited, and deadlines approach quickly, the scope of the test effort must have its limits. The test plan must indicate clearly when testing is complete: If exit criteria are stated in ambiguous terms, the test team cannot determine the point at which the test effort is complete.

For example, a test-completion criterion might be that all defined test procedures, which are based on requirements, have been executed successfully without any significant problems, meaning that all high-priority defects have been fixed by the development staff and verified through regression testing by a member of the test team. Meeting such a criterion, in the context of the other practices discussed throughout this book, provides a high level of confidence that the system meets all requirements without major flaws.

Following are example statements that might be considered as part of exit criteria for an application:

- Test procedures have been executed to determine that the system meets the specified functional and nonfunctional requirements.

- All level 1, level 2, and level 3 (showstopper, urgent, and high-priority) software problems documented as a result of testing have been resolved.

- All level 1 and level 2 (showstopper, urgent) software problems reported have been resolved.

- All level 1 and level 2 (showstopper, urgent) software problems documented as a result of testing have been resolved, and 90 percent of reported level-3 problems have been resolved.

- Software may be shipped with known low-priority defects (and certainly with some unknown defects).

Notwithstanding the exit criteria that have been met, software will be only as successful as it is useful to the customers. Therefore, it is important that user-acceptance testing is factored into the testing plan.

Developers must be made aware of system-acceptance criteria. The test team must communicate the list of entrance and exit criteria to the development staff early on, prior to submitting the test plan for approval. Entrance and exit testing criteria for the organization should be standardized where possible, and based upon criteria that have been proven in several projects.

It may be determined that the system can ship with some defects to be addressed in a later release or a patch. Before going into production, test results can be analyzed to help identify which defects must be fixed immediately versus which can be deferred. For example, some "defect" repairs may be reclassified as enhancements, and then addressed in later software releases. The project or software development manager, together with the other members of the change-control board, are the likely decision-makers to determine whether to fix a defect immediately or risk shipping the product with the defect.

Additional metrics must be evaluated as part of the exit criteria. For example:

- What is the rate of defect discovery in regression tests on previously working functions—in other words, how often are defect fixes breaking previously working functionality?

- How often are defect corrections failing, meaning that a defect thought to be fixed actually wasn't?

- What is the trend in the rate of discovering new defects as this testing phase proceeds? The defect-opening rate should be declining as testing proceeds.

Testing can be considered complete when the application is in an acceptable state to ship or to go live, meeting the exit criteria, even though it most likely contains defects yet to be discovered.

In a world of limited budgets and schedules, there comes a time when testing must halt and the product must be deployed. Perhaps the most difficult decision in software testing is when to stop. Establishing quality guidelines for the completion and release of software will enable the test team to make that decision.

Item 48: Isolate the Test Environment from the Development Environment

t is important that the test environment be set up by the time the testing team is ready to execute the test strategy.

The test environment must be separated from the development environment to avoid costly oversights and untracked changes to the software during testing. Too often, however, this is not the case: To save costs, a separate test environment is not made available for the testing team.

Without a separate test environment, the testing effort is likely to encounter several of the following problems:

- *Changes to the environment.* A developer may apply a fix or other change to the development configuration, or add new data, without informing the testing team. If a tester has just written up a defect based on the environment, that defect may now not be reproducible. The defect report probably must be marked "closed—cannot be reproduced," resulting in wasted development and testing resources. Additionally, unless the developers inform the testers of any changes to existing code made in the course of the day, new defects will be missed. The testers will not know to retest the changed code.

- *Version management.* It's difficult to manage versions when developers and testers share the same environment. Developers may need to integrate new features into the software, while testers need a stable version to complete testing. Conversely, developers usually need somewhere to run the latest build of the software other than their own desktop machines. If testers are sharing the development environment, its resources are less available for use by developers.

- *Changes to the operating environment.* Testing may require reconfiguration of the environment to test the application under various conditions. This creates a large amount of turbulence in the environment, which may impinge upon developer activities. For example, machines may be rebooted, or taken off-line for several days so changes can be made to the installed software or hardware.

While budget constraints often do not allow for a separate testing environment, it is possible that, with certain cost-saving measures, a separate test environment may be created affordably. Some examples:

- *Reduced performance and capacity.* In a testing environment, it may not be necessary to have high-performance machines with massive disk and memory capacity. Smaller machines can be used for most test activities, with results being extrapolated when necessary to estimate performance on larger hardware platforms. This is recommended only if the budget doesn't allow for production-sized test machines, however, as extrapolation is an imprecise way to gauge performance, producing only a ballpark estimate of actual performance in the production environment. When exact numbers are required, performance figures should be derived on production-class hardware.

- *Removable disks.* Testing several configurations does not necessarily require several machines or a complete reinstall for each configuration. A removable disk with multiple partitions allows a single machine to host a multitude of software configurations, saving money and time. See Item 46 for more information on using removable disks for compatibility testing.

- *A shared test lab.* Share the costs of the testing environment by using a test lab for several software projects. The lab should be designed to be easily reconfigured for use with various testing engagements, not so specifically that it works for only one project.

Item 49: Implement a Defect-Tracking Life Cycle

T he defect tracking life cycle is a critical aspect of the testing program. It is important to evaluate and select an adequate defect-tracking tool for the system environment. Once the tool has been acquired, or developed in-house, a defect-tracking life cycle should be instituted, documented, and communicated. All stakeholders must understand the flow of a defect, from the time it has been identified until it has been resolved.

After a defect is fixed, it must be retested. In the defect-tracking system, the element would be labeled as being in **retest status**. The development manager must be aware of and comply with the process for tracking the status of a defect. If the manager did not follow the tracking procedures, how would the test team know which defects to retest?

Test engineers must document the details of a defect and the steps necessary to recreate it, or reference a test procedure if its steps expose the problem, to help the development team pursue its defect-correction activities. Defects are commonly classified based on priority in order that higher-priority defects may be resolved first. Test engineers must participate in change-control boards when those boards are involved in reviewing outstanding defect reports. Once the identified defects have been corrected in a new software build, test engineers are informed via the defect-tracking tool. Testers can then refer to the tracking tool to see which defects are identified as being ready for retesting. Ideally, the record for the fixed defect also contains a description of the fix and what other areas of the system it may affect, helping testers determine which potentially affected areas to also retest.

Each test team must perform defect reporting using a defined process that includes the following steps.

1. ANALYSIS AND DEFECT RECORD ENTRY

The process should describe how to evaluate unexpected system behavior. First, false results must be ruled out. Sometimes a test can produce a false negative, with the system under test behaving as intended but the test incorrectly reporting an error. Or the test (especially when using a testing tool) can produce a false positive, where the system is reported to pass the test when in fact there is an error. The tester must be equipped with specific diagnostic capabilities to determine the accuracy of the test procedure's output.

Assuming the tester's diagnosis determines that the unexpected system behavior is an actual defect (not a false positive, false negative, duplicate of a defect already reported, etc.) a software problem or defect report typically is entered into the defect-tracking tool by a member of the testing team, or by a member of another team who is tasked to report defects.

Following is an example of attributes to be included in documentation of a defect:

- *Subject heading.* The subject heading should start with the name of the system area in which the defect was found—for example, Reports, Security, User Interface, or Database.

- *Version of build under test.* The version number of the build that is being tested. The version should differentiate between production and test builds of the software. Examples: Build #3184, Test_Build_001.

- *Operating system and configuration.* List the operating system and other configuration elements (UNIX, Win98, Win95, WinXP, WinME, Win2000; I.E. 5.5, I.E. 6.0, Netscape 6, and so on) of the test in which the defect was discovered.

- *Attachments.* Examples of attachments are screenshots of the error and printouts of logs. Attachments should be placed in a central repository accessible to all stakeholders.

- *Reproducibility.* Sometimes a defect only occurs intermittently. Indicate whether it's always reproducible, appears inconsistently, or is not reproducible at all.

- *Step-by-step instructions for reproducing the error.* If the error is reproducible, include any information necessary for a developer to reproduce the defect, such as specific data used during the test. The error itself should be clearly described. Avoid vague language such as, "The program displayed incorrect information." Instead, specify the incorrect information the program displayed, as well as the correct information (expected result).

- *Retest failure.* If the defect still appears upon retesting, provide details describing the failure during retest.

- *Category.* The category of behavior being reported may be "defect," "enhancement request," or "change request." The priority of a "change request" or "enhancement request" remains N/A until it is actively being reviewed.

- *Resolution.* Developers are to indicate the corrective action taken to fix the defect.

In reporting defects, **granularity** should be preserved. Each report should cover just one defect. If several defects are interrelated, each should have its own entry, with a cross-reference to the others.

2. PRIORITIZATION

The process must define how to assign a level of priority to each defect. The test engineer initially must assess how serious the problem is to the successful operation of the system. The most critical defects cause software to fail and prevent test activity from continuing. Defects are commonly referred to a change-control board (CCB) for further evaluation and disposition, as discussed in Item 4.

A common defect priority classification scheme is provided below.

1. Showstopper—Testing cannot continue because the defect causes the application to crash, expected functionality is not implemented, and so on.

2. Urgent—Incident is extremely important and requires immediate attention.

3. High—Incident is important and should be resolved as soon as possible after Urgent items.

4. Medium—Incident is important but can be resolved in a reasonably longer time frame because a work-around exists.

5. Low—Incident is not critical and can be resolved as time and resources allow.

6. N/A—Priority is not applicable (e.g., for change and enhancement requests).

Defect priority levels must to be tailored to the project and organization. For some projects, a simple "High/Low" or "High/Medium/Low" system may suffice. Other projects may need many more levels of defect prioritization. However, having too many priority levels makes it difficult to classify defects properly, as the levels begin to lose their distinctiveness and blend together.

3. REOCCURRENCE

The process should define how to handle reoccurring issues. If a defect has been resolved before but continues to reappear, how should it be handled? Should the earlier defect report be reopened, or should a new defect be entered? It is generally advisable to review the earlier defect report to study the implemented fix, but open a new defect report with a cross-reference to the "closed, but related" defect. This style of referencing provides an indication of how often defects are reintroduced after they have been fixed, perhaps pointing to a configuration problem or an issue on the development side.

4. CLOSURE

Once a defect has been corrected, determined to be a duplicate, or deemed not a defect, the report can be closed. However, it should remain in the defect database. No one should delete defect reports from the tracking system. This ensures that all defects and their histories are properly tracked. In addition to the loss of historical information that could prove valuable in the future, deleting records from the defect-tracking system can destroy the continuity of the numbering system. Furthermore, if people have made hard copies of the defect reports, they will not agree with the tracking system file. It is much better practice to simply close the defect by marking it "closed—works as expected," "closed—not a defect," or "closed—duplicate."

It may be useful to have a rule regarding partially corrected defects, such as, "If a defect is only partially fixed, the defect report cannot be closed as fixed." Usually, this should not be an issue. If defect reports are sufficiently detailed and granular, each report will contain only one issue, so there will be no "partially fixed" condition. If multiple problems are encountered, each should be entered in its own defect report, regardless of how similar the problems may be. This way, instead of listing one complex issue as "partially fixed," the elements that are fixed and the elements that are outstanding will each have their own records.

Once a defect has been corrected and unit tested to the satisfaction of the software-development team, the corrected software code is stored in the software configuration management system. At some point, the conclusion is made that an acceptable number of defects has been corrected, or in some cases a single critical defect has been fixed, and a new software build is created and given to the testing team.

Defects are discovered throughout the software development life cycle. It is recommended that the test team generate software problem reports and classify each defect according to the life-cycle phase in which it was found. Table 49.1 provides example categories for software problem reports.

Table 49.1. Categories of Defects and Associated Testing Life Cycle Elements

Category	Applies if a problem has been found in:	System	Software	Hardware
A	System development plan	✔		
B	Operational concept	✔		
C	System or software requirements		✔	✔
D	Design of the system or software		✔	✔
E	The coded software (application under test)		✔	
F	Test plans, cases and procedures report		✔	✔
G	User or support manuals		✔	✔
H	The process being followed on the project		✔	✔
I	Hardware, firmware, communications equipment			✔
J	Any other aspect of the project	✔	✔	✔

When using a defect-tracking tool, the test team must define and document the defect life-cycle model, also called the **defect workflow**. In some organizations, the configuration management group or process engineering group is responsible for the defect workflow, while in other organizations, the test team is responsible. Following is an example of a defect workflow.

Defect Workflow

1. When a defect report is initially generated, its status is set to *"New."*

2. Various teams (test, documentation, product management, development, training, or requirements team) have been designated as being able to open an issue. They select the type of issue:

   -Defect

   -Change Request

   -Enhancement Request

3. The originator then selects the priority of the defect, subject to modification and approved by the change-control board (CCB).

4. A designated party, such as the software manager or the CCB, evaluates the defect, assigns a status, and may modify the issue type and priority.
   The status *"Open"* is assigned to valid defects. The status *"Closed"* is assigned to duplicate defects or user errors. Only the testing team should be allowed to close a defect. The reason for *"closing"* the defect must be documented:

   -Closed: Not Reproducible

   -Closed: Duplicate

   -Closed: Works as expected

   The status *"Enhancement"* is assigned if it's been determined that the reported defect is in fact an enhancement request.

5. If the status is determined to be *"Open,"* the software manager (or other designated person) assigns the defect to the responsible stakeholder, and sets the status to *"Development."*

6. Once the developer begins working on the defect, the status can be set to "*In Development.*"

7. Once the developer believes the defect is fixed, the developer documents the fix in the defect-tracking tool and sets the status to "*Fixed.*" The status can also be set to "*Works As Expected*" or "*Cannot Be Reproduced*" if the software is functioning properly. At the same time, the developer reassigns the defect to the originator.

8. Once a new build is created, the development manager moves all fixed defects contained in the current build to "*re-test*" status.

9. The test engineer re-tests those fixes and other affected areas. If the defect has been corrected with the fix, the test engineer sets the status to "*Closed-Fixed.*" If the defect has not been corrected with the fix, the test engineer sets the status to "*Re-Test Failed.*" If the defect is fixed, but the fix breaks something else in the software a new defect is generated. The cycle repeats.

Item 50: Track the Execution of the Testing Program

E veryone involved in a software project wants to know when testing is completed. To be able to answer that question, it is imperative that test execution be tracked effectively. This is accomplished by collecting data, or metrics, showing the progress of testing. The metrics can help identify when corrections must be made in order to assure success. Additionally, using these metrics the test team can predict a release date for the application. If a release date has been predetermined, the metrics can be used to measure progress toward completion.

Progress metrics are collected iteratively during the stages of the test-execution cycle. Sample progress metrics include the following:

- *Test Procedure Execution Status (%) = executed number of test procedures / total number of test procedures.* This execution status measurement is derived by dividing the number of test procedures already executed by the total number of test procedures planned. By reviewing this metric value, the test team can ascertain the number of percentage of test procedures remaining to be executed. This metric, by itself, does not provide an indication of the quality of the application. It provides information only about the progress of the test effort, without any indication of the success of the testing.

    It is important to measure the test procedure *steps* executed, not just the number of test *procedures* executed. For example, one test procedure may contain 25 steps. If the tester successfully executes Steps 1 through 23, and then encounters a showstopper at Step 24, it is not very informative to report only that the entire test procedure failed; a more useful measurement of progress

255

includes the number of steps executed. Measuring test-procedure execution status at the step level results in a highly granular progress metric.

The best way to track test procedure execution is by developing a matrix that contains the identifier of the build under test, a list of all test procedure names, the tester assigned to each test procedure, and the percentage complete, updated daily and measured by the number of test-procedure steps executed successfully versus total number of test-procedure steps planned. Many test-management or requirements-management tools can help automate this process.

- *Defect Aging = Span from date defect was opened to date defect was closed.* Another important metric in determining progress status is the turnaround time for a defect to be corrected, also called **defect aging**. Defect aging is a high-level metric that verifies whether defects are being addressed in a timely manner. Using defect-aging data, the test team can conduct a trend analysis. For example, suppose 100 defects are recorded for a project. If documented past experience indicates that the development team can fix as many as 20 defects per day, the turnaround time for 100 problem reports may be estimated at one work-week. The defect-aging statistic, in this case, is an average of five days. If the defect-aging measure grows to 10–15 days, the slower response time of the developers making the corrections may affect the ability of the test team to meet scheduled deadlines.

  Standard defect-aging measurement is not always applicable. It sometimes must be modified, depending on the complexity of the specific fix being implemented, among other criteria.

  If developers don't fix defects in time, it can have a ripple effect throughout the project. Testers will run into related defects in another area, creating duplication when one timely fix might have prevented subsequent instances. In addition, the older a defect becomes, the more difficult it may be to correct it, since additional code may be built on top of it. Correcting the defect at a later point may have much larger implications on the software than if it had been corrected when originally discovered.

- *Defect Fix Time to Retest = Span from date defect was fixed and released in new build to date defect was retested.* The defect fix retest metric provides a measure of whether the test team is retesting corrections at an adequate rate. If defects that have been fixed are not retested adequately and in a timely manner, this can hold up progress, since the developer cannot be assured that a fix has not introduced a new defect, or that the original problem has been properly corrected. This last point is especially important: Code that is being developed with the assumption that earlier code has been fixed will have to be reworked if that assumption proves incorrect. If defects are not being retested quickly enough, the testing team must be reminded of the importance of retesting fixes so developers can move forward, knowing their fixes have passed the test.

- *Defect Trend Analysis = Trend in number of defects found as the testing life cycle progresses.* Defect trend analysis can help determine the trend in the identification of defects. Is the trend improving (i.e., are fewer defects being found over time) as the system testing phase is nearing completion, or is the trend worsening? This metric is closely related to "Newly opened defects." The number of newly opened defects should decline as the system-testing phase nears the end. If this is not the case, it may be an indicator of a severely flawed system.

  If the number of defects found increases with each subsequent test release, assuming no new functionality is being delivered and the same code is being tested (changed only by the incorporation of code fixes), several possible causes may be indicated, such as:

  - improper code fixes for previous defects

  - incomplete testing coverage for earlier builds (new testing coverage discovers new defects)

  - inability to execute some tests until some of the defects have been fixed, allowing execution of those tests, which then find new defects

- *Quality of Fixes = Number of errors (newly introduced or reoccurring errors in previously working functionality) remaining per fix.* This metric is also referred to as the **recurrence ratio**. It measures the percentage of fixes that introduce new errors into previously working functionality or break previously working functionality. The value obtained from this calculation provides a measure of the quality of the software corrections implemented in response to problem reports.

  This metric helps the test team determine the degree to which previously working functionality is being adversely affected by software corrections. When this value is high, the test team must make developers aware of the problem.

- *Defect Density = Total number of defects found for a requirement / number of test procedures executed for that requirement.* The defect-density metric is the average number of defects found per test procedure in a specific functional area or requirement. If there is a high defect density in a specific functional area, it is important to conduct a causal analysis using the following types of questions:

  - Is this functionality very complex, and therefore expected to exhibit high defect density?

  - Is there a problem with the design or implementation of the functionality?

  - Were inadequate resources assigned to the functionality, perhaps because its difficulty was underestimated?

  Additionally, when evaluating defect density, the relative priority of the defect must be considered. For example, one application requirement may have as many as 50 low-priority defects and still satisfy acceptance criteria. Another requirement might have one open high-priority defect that prevents the acceptance criteria from being satisfied.

These are just few of the metrics that must be gathered to measure test-program execution; many others are available. The metrics described in this Item are a core set to track in order to identify any need for corrective activity, to highlight risk areas, and ultimately, to enable successful execution of the testing program.

Index

A

Alexander, Christopher, 5
ambiguous requirements, 8
architecture. *See* system architecture.
archive mechanisms, 48
assertions, 104
automated builds
  best practices, 207–209
  unit testing, 156
automated test engineer, 69
automated test tools. *See also* tools.
  application data management, 179
  application incompatibility, 168
  best practices, 175–176
  building *vs.* buying, 167–169
  candidates for, 173–174
  choosing, 175–176
  code-coverage analyzers, 163
  code instrumentors, 163
  cost, 174, 180–181
  coverage, 174, 180

  and development life cycle, 173
  distraction from goals, 175–176
  effects on testing, 171–176
  efficiency, 174
  GUI-testing, 164–165
  help-desk problem reports,
    179–180
  intrusiveness, 175
  load performance, 165
  memory-leak detection, 163
  misconceptions, 172–176
  network-testing, 164
  number required, 172, 179
  operating system incompatibility,
    167–168
  overview, 159–160
  predictability, 175
  reducing test effort, 172–173
  schedules, 173, 180
  scope of testing, 177–178
  specialized, 165

stability requirements, 173
stress testing, 165
summary table of, 162
and system architecture, 178–179
test-data generators, 164
test-management, 164
test-procedure generators, 162–163
testability hooks, 167
testing on prototypes, 183–184
training requirements, 174–175
types of, 161–165
usability-measurement, 163–164
user group discussions, 177
automated testing
    best practices
        automated builds, 207–209
        black-box testing, 187–189
        capture/playback tools, 187–189
        data-driven frameworks, 197
        developing test scripts, 197–200
        establishing a start point,
            194–195
        hard-coded data values, 187–188
        managing test results, 195
        modular script development, 198
        modular user-interface navigation,
            198–199
        non-modular scripts, 188
        pre-built libraries, 199–200
        regression testing, 201–205
        reusability, 188–189
        reusable functions, 199–200
        smoke tests, 207–209
        test-case management, 193–195
        test harnesses, 191–195
        version control, 200
    candidates for, 113
    designing tests, 113

B

back-end testing *vs.* GUI, 31–32
baselining requirements, 16
beta products, testing, 41
black-box testing
    best practices, 187–189
    definition, 91
    vs. gray-box, 111
    path analysis, 130
boundary-value (BV) analysis, 44, 131
budgets. *See also* costs.
    automated test tools, 180–181
    planning, 28, 40
buffer overflow attacks, 225
builds
    automated, 156
    planning, 60
    unit test, 155–157
business processing layer, 147
BV (boundary-value) analysis, 44, 131

C

capture/playback tools, 112, 187–189
CCB (Change Control Board), 15, 16
Change Control Board (CCB), 15, 16
change management
    baselining, 16
    CCB (Change Control Board), 16
    change-request forms, 16
    communicating changes, 15–17
    Engineering Review Board, 15
    outdated documentation, 15–17
    requirement-change process, 16
    requirements-managing tools, 17
    software defects, 16
    tracking changes, 17
    undocumented changes, 15

change-request forms, 16
code-coverage analyzers, 163
code instrumentors, 163
code layers, 146–149
commercial off-the-shelf (COTS)
    tools, 112
compatibility testing, 235–237
Competitive Engineering, 5
competitive evaluations, 222
compiling, unit testing in local versions,
    155–157
completeness of requirements, 6–7
component testing. *See* unit testing.
concurrency protection, 230–233
concurrency testing, 229–233
configuring logging, 105–106
consistency of requirements, 7
constraints, in test procedures, 135–137
corporate culture, effects on testing, 27
correctness of requirements, 6
costs. *See also* budgets.
    automated test tools, 174
    early defect correction, 4
    over development life cycle, 4
COTS (commercial off-the-shelf)
    tools, 112
coverage. *See also* scope of testing.
    automated test tools, 174, 180
    code-coverage analyzers, 163
    data flow, 43
    planning tests, 25, 34
    source code coverage analysis, 180
    test, 25, 34
critical requirements
    designing tests, 124
    mission-critical applications, 60
customers. *See also* users.
    environment, 48
    expectations, 27
    needs, 39

D
data dictionaries, 43
data-driven frameworks, 197
data element details in test procedures,
    135–137
data flow coverage, 43
data for tests. *See* test data.
data values, hard-coded, 187–188
database abstraction layer, 146–147
debug build, 104
debug-information-level logging,
    105–106
debug mode, 103–106
debugging
    with logs, 103–106
    removing, 104–105
defect trend analysis, 257
Defect Workflow, 88
defects
    aging, 256
    analyzing
        Defect Workflow, 88–89
        false negatives, 94–95
        false positives, 94–95
        fix-time to retest, 256
        as measure of tester effectiveness,
        84–87
        recurrence ratio, 257
        system architecture, 93–95
    density, 258
    managing test results, 195
    prevention, requirements phase, 3
    tracking life cycle
        closure, 250–253
        defect attributes, 248–249
        defect categories, 251
        defect workflow, 252–253
        documenting defects, 248–249
        granularity, 249
        overview, 247–248

prioritization, 249–250
reoccurrence, 250
retest status, 247
design documentation, 43
design standards, 115–119
designing tests. *See also* planning tests;
    test procedures.
  automation, 113
  black-box *vs.* gray-box, 111
  critical requirements, 124
  design standards, 115–119
  divide-and-conquer strategy, 110–114
  exploratory testing, 139–141
  high-risk requirements, 124
  methodology, 110
  nonfunctional tests, 118–119
  personnel, 110
  procedure templates, 115–119
  prototyping, 127–128
  reviewing the design plan, 123
  scope of testing, 109
  techniques for, 129–133
  test-case scenarios, 129–133
  test cases, 121–124
  test data, 114
  test harnesses, 111–112
  test sequence, 109–110, 123
  testing techniques, 112, 129–133
  tools, 112
  without requirements, 111
developer-to-engineer ratio, 52–53
development
  based on existing systems, 19–22
    development process, 22
    documenting existing application, 21
    documenting updates, 21–22
    estimating resources, 20
    managing expectations, 21–22
    "moving target" environment, 20

overview, 19–20
    pros and cons, 20
    using fixed versions, 21
  unit testing, 144–149
Development Ratio Method, 52–53
divide-and-conquer strategy, 110–114
documentation. *See also* requirements.
  change management, 15–17
  defect tracking, 248–249
  existing systems, 21–22
  functional requirements, 6
  living documents, 125–126
  nonfunctional requirements, 7, 216
  requirements
    outdated documentation, 15–17
    undocumented changes, 15
    use cases, 6
  test procedures
    constraints, 135–137
    designing, 11–14
    documenting, 117–118, 125–126
    estimating number of, 54–56
    and team size, 54–56
domain object layer, 147

E

early involvement
  requirements phase, 3–4
  test planning, 27
effort level, estimating
  factors affecting, 58–60
  importance of, 28
  number of tasks, 56–58
  number of test procedures, 54–56
  Task Planning method, 56–58
  Test Procedure method, 54–56
engineer-to-developer ratio, 52–53
Engineering Review Board, 15

equipment purchase list, 49
equivalence partitioning, 130
error cases, 149
error-level logging, 105–106
estimating
  based on existing systems, 20
  effort level
    factors affecting, 58–60
    importance of, 28
    number of tasks, 56–58
    number of test procedures, 54–56
    Task Planning method, 56–58
    Test Procedure method, 54–56
  personnel hours, 56–58
  team size
    developer to engineer ratio, 52–53
    Development Ratio Method, 52–53
    number of tasks, 56–58
    number of test procedures, 54–56
    Project Staff Ratio method, 53–54
    Task Planning method, 56–58
    Test Procedure method, 54–56
    total project requirements, 53–54
  time
    Task Planning method, 56–58
    WBS (work breakdown structure), 52
exceptions, 149
experience levels of testers, 76
exploratory testing, 139–141
extreme programming, 151

F

false negatives, 94–95
false positives, 94–95
feasibility of requirements, 7
features, prioritizing, 39–40
field studies, 222

focus groups, 221–222
functional analysis, 130
functional test tools, 112, 187–189
functional *vs.* nonfunctional
    requirements, 26–27
    testing, 82–83
functions, reusing, 199–200. *See
    also* methods.

G

Gilb, Tom, 5
global nonfunctional constraints, 216
gray-box testing
  vs. black-box, 111
  definition, 41, 91
  problem types, 94–95
GUI testing. *See also* user interface.
  automated test tools, 164–165
  vs. back-end testing, 31–32

H

hard-coded data values, 187–188
hardware requirements, 48
help-desk problem reports, 179–180
high-risk requirements, 124

I

in-bounds data, 131
interface-based unit testing, 152
iterations, 13
iterative development process, 13

K

keystrokes, recording, 164–165

L

libraries, reusable functions, 199–200
living documents, 125–126
load performance tools, 165
lock acquisition, 232
lock enforcement, 232
lock release, 232
locking data, 230–233
log contents, 99–101
logging. *See also* tracking test execution.
    configuring, 105–106
    debug-information level, 105–106
    as debugging tool, 103–106
    error level, 105–106
    increasing testability, 99–101
    source code, inspecting, 103

M

maintainability, test procedures, 135–137
managing test results, 195
manual test engineer, 68
memory-leak detection tools, 163
methods, 99. *See also* functions.
mission-critical applications, 60
"moving target" environment, 20
multi-user data access, 229–233

N

necessity of requirements, 7
negative testing, 131
network characteristics, 48
network test engineer, 69
network-testing tools, 164
nonfunctional requirements
    documentation, 7, 216
    vs. functional, 26–27
nonfunctional testing
    compatibility testing, 235–237

concurrency testing, 229–233
    designing, 118–119
    examples, 214–215
    vs. functional, 82–83
    global nonfunctional constraints, 216
    identifying the target audience, 221–223
    locking data, 230–233
    multi-user access, 229–233
    performance testing, 217–219
    planning, 213–216
    risks, 215–216
    security, 225–227
    test data, 217–219
    usability testing, 221–223
Notes On the Synthesis of Form, 5

O

on-bounds data, 131
online resources
    automated tools, 198
    user group discussions, 177
optimistic locking, 230–233
orthogonal array testing, 112
orthogonal arrays, 132–133
out-of-bounds data, 131

P

pass/fail unit testing criteria, 157
patches, 42
path analysis, 130
performance testing, 217–219
personnel. *See also* teams.
    designing tests, 110
    estimating hours, 56–58
    required, 33, 40
pessimistic locking, 230–233
phased solutions, 28
phases of testing, 34

Planguage, 5
planning tests. *See also* designing tests;
    test procedures.
  archive mechanisms, 48
  assumptions, 31
  beta products, 41
  budget, 28, 40
  complexity, 39
  corporate culture, 27
  coverage, 25, 34
  customer environment, 48
  customer expectations, 27
  customer needs, 39
  defects, 42
  design techniques, 33
  developing test harnesses or scripts, 33
  early involvement, 27
  environment, 47–49
  equipment purchase list, 49
  estimating effort level
    factors affecting, 58–60
    importance of, 28
    number of tasks, 56–58
    number of test procedures, 54–56
    Task Planning method, 56–58
    Test Procedure method, 54–56
  estimating personnel hours, 56–58
  estimating team size
    developer to engineer ratio, 52–53
    Development Ratio Method, 52–53
    number of tasks, 56–58
    number of test procedures, 54–56
    Project Staff Ratio method, 53–54
    Task Planning method, 56–58
    Test Procedure method, 54–56
    total project requirements, 53–54
  expertise required, 33
  features, prioritizing, 39–40
  functional *vs.* nonfunctional
    requirements, 26–27
  goals, 25–29
  gray-box testing, 41
  GUI *vs.* back-end testing, 31–32
  hardware requirements, 48
  mission-critical applications, 60
  network characteristics, 48
  nonfunctional, 213–216
  number of builds, 60
  patches, 42
  personnel required, 33, 40
  phased solutions, 28
  phases, 34
  pre-release products, 41
  prerequisites, 31
  process definition, 60
  production environment, 47–49
  release criteria, 25, 34
  results expectations, 27
  results of previous tests, 28
  reviewing the plan, 123
  risks
    assessing, 36–37
    factors affecting, 35–36
    mitigating, 36–37
    prioritizing, 35, 39
  schedules, 28, 34, 59, 60
  service packs, 42
  software issues, 41–42
  software requirements, 48
  solution type, 28
  staged implementation, 42
  strategies, 26, 31–34
  system architecture, 31
  technology choices, 28, 41–42
  test data
    breadth, 45
    BV (boundary-value) analysis,
     44, 131
    conditions tested, 46
    data dictionaries, 43

data flow coverage, 43
depth, 44
design documentation, 43
in-bounds data, 131
integrity, 45
on-bounds data, 131
out-of-bounds data, 131
preparation, 46
representative data samples, 133
scope, 45
time estimation
    Task Planning method, 56–58
    WBS (work breakdown structure), 52
tools, 33, 59
understanding the requirements,
    26–29
pre-release products, testing, 41
prioritization of requirements, 8
prioritizing
features, 39–40
requirements, 8
risks, 35, 39
production environment, 47–49
progress tracking, 255–258
Project Staff Ratio method, 53–54
prototyping
designing tests, 127–128
testing automated test tools, 183–184
publications
    Competitive Engineering, 5
    Notes On the Synthesis of Form, 5
pure unit testing, 144

Q

quality checklist, 6–9
quality measures, 5

R

Rational Software Corporation, 35
recording keystrokes, 164–165
regression testing
automated, best practices, 201–205
release criteria, 25, 34
release mode, 103–106
reporting defects. *See* defects, analyzing.
representative data samples, 133
requirement-change process, 16
requirements. *See also* documentation.
ambiguity, 8
based on existing systems
    development process, 22
    documenting existing application, 21
    documenting updates, 21–22
    estimating resources, 20
    managing expectations, 21–22
    "moving target" environment, 20
    overview, 19–20
    pros and cons, 20
    using fixed versions, 21
completeness, 6–7
consistency, 7
correctness, 6
definition, 6
documenting, 6
feasibility, 7
functional *vs.* nonfunctional, 26–27
iterative development process, 13
necessity, 7
prioritization, 8
quality checklist, 6–9
quality measures, 5
reward/penalty technique, 8
testability, 3, 7, 12–13
traceability, 8–9

understanding, 26–29
use cases, 6
verifiability, 7
verifying, 5–9
waterfall development model, 13
requirements, nonfunctional
documentation steps, 7
requirements-managing tools, 17
requirements phase
change management
baselining, 16
CCB (Change Control Board), 16
change-request forms, 16
communicating changes, 15–17
Engineering Review Board, 15
outdated documentation, 15–17
requirement-change process, 16
requirements-managing tools, 17
software defects, 16
tracking changes, 17
undocumented changes, 15
defect prevention, 3
designing test procedures, 11–14
tester involvement, 3–4
Requirements-Services-Interfaces (RSI)
unit testing, 152
results. *See* defects.
reviewing plans, 123
reward/penalty requirements
technique, 8
risks
assessing, 36–37
factors affecting, 35–36
high-risk requirements, 124
mitigating, 36–37
nonfunctional tests, 215–216
prioritizing, 35, 39
RSI (Requirements-Services-Interfaces)
unit testing, 152

S

scenarios
designing tests, 129–133
spreadsheets, 136
schedules
automated test tools, 173, 180
entrance criteria, 241–243
establishing a start point, 194–195
exit criteria, 241–243
planning, 28, 34, 59, 60
scope of testing. *See also* coverage.
automated test tools, 177–178
designing tests, 109
test data, 45
scripts
developing, 33
developing, best practices, 197–200
modular development, best
practices, 198
non-modular, best practices, 188
recording keystrokes, 164–165
security
buffer overflow attacks, 225
locking data, 230–233
nonfunctional tests, 225–227
security test engineer, 70
service packs, 42
SMEs (subject-matter experts)
identifying the target audience, 221
role in test team, 75–76
smoke tests, 204, 207–209
software builds
automating, 156
best practices, 207–209
build process, 156
debug build, 104
planning, 60
sequence of events, 208–209
unit test, 155–157

software issues, 41–42
software requirements, 48
source code, inspecting, 103
source code coverage analysis, 180
staged implementation, 42
strategies, 26, 31–34
strength, orthogonal arrays, 133
stress-testing tools, 165
stubbed components, 144, 152–154
subject-matter experts (SMEs)
    identifying the target audience, 221
    role in test team, 75–76
surveys, 222
system architecture
    automated test tools, 178–179
    debug mode, 103–106
    defect reporting, 93–95
    overview, 91
    release mode, 103–106
    risk analysis, 31
    testability, 97–98
    underlying components, 93–95

T

Task Planning method, 56–58
teams. *See also* testers.
    early involvement, 3–4, 27
    effectiveness, evaluating
        attention to detail, 84
        defect analysis, 84–86, 87, 88–89
        development phase, 84
        experienced testers *vs.* novices, 82
        feedback, 87
        following instructions, 84
        functional *vs.* nonfunctional testing,
            82–83
        overview, 64, 79–80
        self evaluations, 86–90
        setting goals, 80–81

SMEs *vs.* technical experts, 81–82
        tester comments, 88–89
        testing phase, 83–84
    roles and responsibilities
        automated test engineer, 69
        experience levels, 76
        manual test engineer, 68
        network test engineer, 69
        sample team structure, 71–73
        security test engineer, 70
        skills mix, 75–77
        SMEs (subject matter experts),
            75–76
        technical expertise, 76
        technical leader, 67
        technical testers, 76
        test environment specialist, 70
        test library and configuration
            specialist, 70
        test manager, 66
        usability test engineer, 68
        work packages, 65–66
    size, estimating
        developer to engineer ratio, 52–53
        Development Ratio Method, 52–53
        number of tasks, 56–58
        number of test procedures, 54–56
        Project Staff Ratio method, 53–54
        Task Planning method, 56–58
        Test Procedure method, 54–56
        total project requirements, 53–54
technical expertise of testers, 76
technical leader, 67
technical testers, 76
techniques
    definition, 193–194
    for designing tests, 112, 129–133
techniques for designing tests, 129–133
technology choices, 28, 41–42
templates for test procedures, 135–137

test cases
   designing tests, 121–124
   managing, 193–195
   scenarios
      designing tests, 129–133
      spreadsheets, 136
test data
   breadth, 45
   BV (boundary-value) analysis, 44, 131
   conditions tested, 46
   data dictionaries, 43
   data flow coverage, 43
   depth, 44
   design documentation, 43
   designing tests, 114
   in-bounds data, 131
   integrity, 45
   nonfunctional tests, 217–219
   on-bounds data, 131
   out-of-bounds data, 131
   preparation, 46
   randomly generated, 218
   representative data samples, 133
   scope, 45
test-data generators, 164
test environment
   capacity, 246
   change management, 245
   isolating from development
      environment, 245–246
   operating environment, 246
   performance, 246
   removable disks, 246
   shared labs, 246
   version management, 245–246
test environment specialist, 70
test-harness adapters, 192
test harnesses
   best practices, 191–195
   designing tests, 111–112
   developing, 33

test library and configuration
      specialist, 70
test-management tools, 164
test manager, 66
test plan. *See* designing tests; planning tests.
test-procedure generators, 162–163
Test Procedure method, 54–56
test procedures. *See also* designing tests;
      documentation; planning tests;
      requirements.
   constraints, 135–137
   data element details, 135–137
   designing, 11–14
   documenting, 117–118, 125–126
   entrance criteria, 241–243
   estimating number of, 54–56
   exit criteria, 241–243
   as living documents, 125–126
   maintainability, 135–137
   standard contents, 117–118
   and team size, 54–56
   templates, 115–119, 135–137
   test-scenario spreadsheets, 136
test results. *See* defects.
test-scenario spreadsheets, 136
test sequence
   designing tests, 109–110, 123
test shells, 204
test teams. *See* teams.
testability
   increasing with logs, 99–101
   verifying, 97–98
testability hooks, 167
testability of requirements, 3, 7, 12–13
testers. *See also* teams.
   early involvement, 3–4, 27
   technical expertise, 76
testing. *See also* designing tests; planning
      tests; test procedures.
   automated test tools on prototypes,
      183–184

based on existing systems
    development process, 22
    documenting existing application, 21
    documenting updates, 21–22
    estimating resources, 20
    managing expectations, 21–22
    "moving target" environment, 20
    overview, 19–20
    pros and cons, 20
    using fixed versions, 21
coverage. *See also* scope of testing.
    automated test tools, 174, 180
    code-coverage analyzers, 163
    data flow, 43
    planning tests, 25, 34
    source code coverage analysis, 180
    test, 25, 34
techniques
    definition, 193–194
    for designing tests, 112, 129–133
testing quality into a product, 26
time estimation
    Task Planning method, 56–58
    WBS (work breakdown structure), 52
tools. *See also* automated test tools.
    capture/playback, 112, 187–189
    COTS (commercial off-the-shelf), 112
    debugging, 103–106
    designing tests, 112
    enterprise level, 207
    functional test, 112, 187–189
    planning tests, 33, 59
    process management, 207
    requirements-managing, 17
    in test design, 112
traceability of requirements, 8–9
tracking test execution, 255–258. *See
        also* logging.
training requirements, automated test
        tools, 174–175

U

unit-test frameworks, 157
unit testing
    automated builds, 156
    in the build process, 155–157
    business processing layer, 147
    code layers, 146–149
    compiling in local versions, 155–157
    database abstraction layer, 146–147
    in the development process,
        144–149
    domain object layer, 147
    error cases, 149
    before implementation, 151–154
    interface-based approach, 152
    missing components. *See* stubbed
        components.
    overview, 143–144
    parallel to implementation, 151–154
    pass/fail criteria, 157
    path analysis, 130
    pure, 144
    RSI (Requirements-Services-Interfaces)
        approach, 152
    standardization, 156–157
    stubbed components, 144, 152–154
    unit-test frameworks, 157
    user interface layer, 147
    user interfaces *vs.* component or
        software interfaces, 152
usability
    definition, 68
    identifying the target audience, 222
    measurement tools, 163–164
    testing, 221–223
usability test engineer, 68
use cases, 6
user interface
    vs. component or software
        interfaces, 152

GUI testing
   automated test tools, 164–165
   vs. back-end testing, 31–32
   modular navigation, best practices,
      198–199
user interface layer, 147
users. *See also* customers.
   identifying the target audience, 221–223
   needs analysis
      field studies, 222
      focus groups, 221–222
      online group discussions, 177
      surveys, 222

V

verifying requirements, 5–9
version control, 200

W

waterfall development model, 13
white-box testing, 130, 187–189
work packages, 65–66
wrap up, 188
wrappers, 204

Also Available from Addison-Wesley

Automated Software Testing
Introduction, Management, and Performance
Elfriede Dustin, Jeff Rashka, John Paul

With the urgent demand for rapid turnaround on new software releases—without compromising quality—the testing element of application development must keep pace, requiring a major shift from slow, labor-intensive testing methods to a faster and more thorough automated testing approach. *Automated Software Testing* is a comprehensive, step-by-step guide to the most effective tools, techniques, and methods for automated testing. Using numerous case studies of successful industry implementations, this book presents everything you need to know to successfully incorporate automated testing into the development process.

0-201-43287-0 • Paperback • 608 pages • © 1999

Quality Web Systems
Performance, Security, and Usability
Elfriede Dustin, Jeff Rashka, Douglas McDiarmid

Today's Web software professionals must deliver new Web applications to market quickly, while incorporating proper functionality, ease-of-use, security, and performance. This pressure underscores the need for effective engineering that facilitates both quality and rapid Web system development. *Quality Web Systems* provides Web developers and software test professionals with practical, experience-based guidance on Web system engineering. Concise and straightforward, this book provides a framework for ensuring that key Web system success criteria are addressed during the development of the Web system. Detailed, technical guidance is provided for each success criteria, including testing strategies that allow for verification of a quality implementation.

0-201-71936-3 • Paperback • 352 pages • © 2002

inform IT